W9-BTI-819

Learning in Groups

Clark Bouton, Russell Y. Garth, *Editors*

NEW DIRECTIONS FOR TEACHING AND LEARNING
KENNETH E. EBLE and JOHN F. NOONAN, *Editors-in-Chief*
Number 14, June 1983

Paperback sourcebooks in
The Jossey-Bass Higher Education Series

Jossey-Bass Inc., Publishers
San Francisco • Washington • London

Clark Bouton, Russell Y. Garth (Eds.).
Learning in Groups.
New Directions for Teaching and Learning, no. 14.
San Francisco: Jossey-Bass, 1983.

New Directions for Teaching and Learning Series
Kenneth E. Eble and John F. Noonan, *Editors-in-Chief*

New Directions for Teaching and Learning is published quarterly
by Jossey-Bass Inc., Publishers. Subscriptions, single-issue
orders, change of address notices, undelivered copies, and other
correspondence should be sent to *New Directions* Subscriptions,
Jossey-Bass Inc., Publishers, 433 California Street, San Francisco,
California 94104.

Editorial correspondence should be sent to the Editors-in-Chief,
Kenneth E. Eble or John F. Noonan, Center for Improving
Teaching Effectiveness, Virginia Commonwealth University,
Richmond, Virginia 23284.

Library of Congress Catalogue Card Number LC 82-84208
International Standard Serial Number ISSN 0271-0633
International Standard Book Number ISBN 87589-974-9

Cover art by Willi Baum
Manufactured in the United States of America

Ordering Information

The paperback sourcebooks listed below are published quarterly and can be ordered either by subscription or single-copy.

Subscriptions cost $35.00 per year for institutions, agencies, and libraries. Individuals can subscribe at the special rate of $21.00 per year *if payment is by personal check.* (Note that the full rate of $35.00 applies if payment is by institutional check, even if the subscription is designated for an individual.) Standing orders are accepted. Subscriptions normally begin with the first of the four sourcebooks in the current publication year of the series. When ordering, please indicate if you prefer your subscription to begin with the first issue of the *coming* year.

Single copies are available at $7.95 when payment accompanies order, and *all single-copy orders under $25.00 must include payment.* (California, New Jersey, New York, and Washington, D.C., residents please include appropriate sales tax.) For billed orders, cost per copy is $7.95 plus postage and handling. (Prices subject to change without notice.)

Bulk orders (ten or more copies) of any individual sourcebook are available at the following discounted prices: 10–49 copies, $7.15 each; 50–100 copies, $6.35 each; over 100 copies, *inquire.* Sales tax and postage and handling charges apply as for single copy orders.

To ensure correct and prompt dvlivery, all orders must give either the *name of an individual* or an *official purchase order number.* Please submit your order as follows:

Subscriptions: specify series and year subscription is to begin.
Single Copies: specify sourcebook code (such as, TL8) and first two words of title.

Mail orders for United States and Possessions, Latin America, Canada, Japan, Australia, and New Zealand to:
Jossey-Bass Inc., Publishers
433 California Street
San Francisco, California 94104

Mail orders for all other parts of the world to:
Jossey-Bass Limited
28 Banner Street
London EC1Y 8QE

New Directions for Teaching and Learning Series
Kenneth E. Eble and John F. Noonan, *Editors-in-Chief*

Contents

Editors' Notes

At one time or another, most teachers have asked students in a course to form groups in which to discuss topics or do a project. A group exercise can offer a break from the usual lecture, laboratory, or "I'll take questions" routine. For the most part, however, group activities have remained merely an adjunct of the collegiate educational experience.

This *New Directions* sourcebook focuses on some intriguing examples in which group activity is the principal or exclusive process in a college course, not a supplement to the usual lecture-and-discussion method. We have chosen to call them *learning groups*. To ensure active participation by all members, learning groups are kept small—between two and seven members. Often, groups are permanent for the duration of a semester. Teachers are rarely full-time members; instead, they assist groups to establish and achieve learning goals. Each group pursues its various learning tasks in its own way.

Origin of this Sourcebook

This sourcebook has its origin in the portfolio of grants made over the past several years by the U.S. Department of Education's Fund for the Improvement of Postsecondary Education (FIPSE).

Fund staff noticed that several projects had use of learning groups in common. Like individualized and self-directed learning, internships and other forms of experiential learning, and interactive uses of electronic technology, use of learning groups seemed to cause more active modes of learning, since students were able to assume greater control over what they learned and how they learned it. Beginning in 1980, the Fund solicited proposals under the rubric *active learning* and mentioned group learning as a particular interest. A number of the examples reported in this book began with Fund support.

Interestingly, the use of learning groups was often not seen by teachers as the basic description of what they were doing, since learning groups were usually only part of a larger instructional strategy. These teachers were trying to teach writing, improve medical practice in rural areas, or encourage faculty to think more seriously about the nature of their teaching. They saw themselves as using problem-solving techniques, as putting the learner first, or as making the student

1

think. They were all using learning groups, but they did not all see that that was the key to the success that they were having.

The authors of the chapters in this volume met in Washington, D.C., in March 1982 to discuss whether the idea of learning groups had any power and utility as an organizing concept for the kinds of educating that they had been doing. The decision to develop this book indicates that the answer was affirmative. Most of us had not known each other beforehand, yet we discovered that we shared not only many techniques and practices but also many assumptions.

We also decided to use the term *learning group* as a general rubric, recognizing that a variety of labels are in use for such activity: *cooperative learning, collaborative learning, collective learning, study circles, team learning, partner learning, study groups, peer support groups, work groups, learning community, self-help groups,* and *community education circles.*

Structure of this Sourcebook

The authors of the chapters in this book began to use learning groups as a way to solve a difficult and persistent problem within higher education. These problems form the organizing principle of this volume. Chapters One through Seven describe the various types of learning groups developed on individual campuses to address such problems as overcoming student passivity in large classes (Monk, Michaelsen), developing liberal education skills and abilities (Bouton and Rice), teaching writing (Bruffee), developing competent professionals (Michaelsen and Obenshain), improving scholarly ability among graduate students (Maimon), and encouraging learning beyond the classroom (Osborne).

Chapters Eight and Nine discuss common themes in the diverse experiences of the author. Both chapters reflect discussions at the authors' meeting in Washington. Perhaps the most striking theme that emerged from those discussions is the evidence for enhanced learning across a broad front — at diverse institutions, in different disciplines, with varying student populations. After all, any claim of educational improvement ultimately depends on actual evidence of learning.

A second point made by these two chapters is that learning groups seem to have two major elements: first, a process of group conversation and activity that promotes active learning (Chapter Eight); second, a way for faculty to guide this learning process and to offer their expertise by structuring tasks or activities (Chapter Nine). Neither element is radically new for higher education, but in combination they seem to be considerably more powerful than either used alone is. The process of group conversation assumes that learners must construct knowledge for themselves, not receive it fully formed from an instructor. Similarly, a teacher's development of tasks for students assumes that teaching is not a single and unvarying role but that it consists of functions that can be rearranged in time and emphasis.

Learning Groups in Society

Although this volume focuses on the use of learning groups in colleges, such use has wider implications. The purest and, in some ways, the most interesting learning groups arise beyond academic borders. Purposes — a work task, peer support, team building — sometimes overshadow learning goals, yet learning is frequently both an intended and an actual result. For example, study circles, sometimes simply called *circles,* have flourished for years in this country, often sponsored by churches or community organizations. Within workplaces and community organizations, members of work groups formed to solve a particular problem collectively sometimes also begin to explore the real individual learning that also occurs. Women's support groups, a major element of the women's movement of the past fifteen years, illustrate another version. Sensitivity, encounter, and T groups have been a key technique for the human potential movement; they demonstrate that groups can move beyond cognitive learning. Other types of group learning, such as team building, have been important for the field of organizational development. There have been other, more temporary and less structured uses: the freedom schools that arose spontaneously during the civil rights marches in the South in the 1960s, and the Vietnam War teach-ins on college campuses, which, in their own way, went equally beyond the academic mainstream. Although it is beyond the scope of this book, greater attention to the learning potential of all group efforts could be quite important. It is possible, in fact, that a concern with college-based learning groups could promote efforts to understand the common elements of learning groups throughout society.

The Significance of Learning Groups

The authors of the chapters in this volume think that the potential of learning groups has yet to be realized. Some standard objections and myths about learning groups have prompted a number of questions about this type of learning: Can learning groups cover as much material as the standard lecture-discussion method? Will learning groups work in disciplines, such as mathematics and hard science, where discussion does not seem so important? How can students teach each other when they do not know as much as the teacher? What structures this method of teaching? Does it give feelings too prominent a role? What happens to the teacher's expertise?

The authors have answers to these questions. To start with, learning groups work — that is, they enhance learning — irrespective of the type of institution, type of student, level of education, or subject matter. Indeed, learning groups promote the broad liberal education goals that are often more honored by educational rhetoric than pursued in classroom practice — specific information and content, general disciplinary concepts, generic cognitive abilities, interpersonal skills, knowledge about higher education communities, and understanding of how to learn. Learning groups seem to increase both the efficiency and the effectiveness of learning. (See particularly Chapters One and Two, on large classes.) Learning groups have also sparked many faculty members, including the authors, to reassess their teaching.

It is possible to see connections with more expansive notions. For example, some teachers are beginning to make the case for a collaborative or social theory of knowledge. (Chapter Eight touches on this point.) Learning groups can also be seen in the context of major academic trends. There are signs now of serious attention to shared learning needs and to common or even required core curricula. Learning groups seem to offer both a real and a symbolically important way of structuring educational experiences so as to promote shared and common learning. Finally, learning groups can be tried without sizable new resources and without major alterations in university structure.

The time seems right for an increase in the use of learning groups. Recently, college campuses have revealed a seriousness about teaching that has not been much in evidence since research became so important to higher education. A variety of disciplinary endeavors in cognitive psychology, epistemology, history of science, and sociology of knowledge have provided new understandings of the nature of learning and knowledge. Under these circumstances, learning groups may find wider use in higher education than they did at other periods of high interest in group approaches, such as the 1950s and 1960s. The authors of the chapters in this book play a twofold part in trying to encourage greater use of learning groups. First, they have tried to understand the phenomenon a little better themselves. Second, they seek here to share some of that understanding with others.

Clark Bouton
Russell Y. Garth
Editors

Clark Bouton is a professor of sociology at the University of the District of Columbia. He has written, led workshops, and received grants to study the use of learning groups in college teaching.

Russell Y. Garth, program officer with the U.S. Department of Education's Fund for the Improvement of Postsecondary Education, has worked with several projects that experimented with learning groups. Earlier, he was assistant to the president at the University of Santa Clara and staff member for a higher education committee of the California legislature.

Active student engagement in a large lecture course seems to be a contradiction in terms. How can the power of the teacher in this setting be used to remove the apparent conflict?

Student Engagement and Teacher Power in Large Classes

G. Stephen Monk

I was mildly flattered when I was asked to teach a large lecture course, since I was also faintly attracted by the power of having an effect, all at once, on 350 young minds. The request indicated that I had joined a circle of competent teachers in my department who could give the clear explanations that a large lecture demands; who are sufficiently well organized, patient, and self-assured to get the subject across to a large, diverse audience; and who are free of the idiosyncrasies of style that are charming in a teacher with a few students but disastrous in a teacher with many. For my part, I viewed this course as an opportunity to be a success as a teacher on a new, grand scale. I would not have time to do grading or to hold routine office hours, but I would stay in close contact with the course by directing the work of my five teaching assistants (TAs). The bulk of my effort was committed to the task of planning, polishing, and delivering three lectures a week.

Looking back to that time, I view my attempt to express my teacherly impulses as a lecturer in a large course as roughly parallel to attempts to express sensitivity for the less fortunate of our society as a county jailer. My first discovery was that I had no real power in the lec-

C. Bouton and R. Y. Garth (Eds.). *Learning in Groups.* New Directions for
Teaching and Learning, no. 14. San Francisco: Jossey-Bass, June 1983.

ture room, unless I counted the capacity to cause 350 people to copy a steady stream of words and symbols into their notebooks as a sign of real power. Any sense that I had had in the past of affecting my students' minds was based on interaction with them. But interactions are maintained by a wide variety of overt and covert social devices, and most of these seemed unavailable or inappropriate in the large lecture room. With just three hours a week in which to get my points across, I felt that not a minute of class time should be wasted. My lectures were highly polished performances meant to be transcribed in class and studied by students on their own time. After a while, I disciplined myself to stop to ask questions of the students or to solicit questions from them, but my requests met a chilling silence. The students were so busy transcribing my lectures that they did not have time to ask questions or to formulate answers of their own.

What of my staff of five teaching assistants? They were in charge of the quiz sections, where the students were to be actively engaged, and I was in charge of them. At first, we had regular staff meetings to discuss issues that came up in the course, but these meetings never progressed beyond purely administrative matters. Then, I began to type up one- to two-page memos describing my lectures and outlining the material to be covered in quiz sections. I continued this practice until the second time I saw a TA deposit my memo in a wastebasket after a cursory look. Later, I learned that TAs, like sergeants in the army, see superiors with bright ideas come and go. They are close to the troops and they know what is best for them. My TAs knew that I was required to follow the textbook, so each TA followed it in his or her own way and ignored me. Far from being my agents to the students, they saw themselves as protecting "their" students against me.

The predicament that I was in would horrify any teacher who cares about students' intellectual growth. But it was much more horrifying for me, because I teach mathematics. Any mathematician will tell you that there is only one way to learn mathematics, and that is to do mathematics. From what I knew about my own lectures and from what I gathered about quiz sections and office hours, my TAs and I spent all the course time telling students how we did mathematics. Their job was to imitate us when they did the homework. The message was that learning was to take place not on course time, but on their own time, away from teachers and away from one another.

The same vanity that led me to accept this teaching assignment propelled me to try to get students more actively engaged. It was intolerable to fill a room with my own talk and get so little response. I reasoned that I did not have to say everything that students needed to know, because it was clearly displayed in the text. So, I adopted an approach to my lectures in which students and I worked simple problems together. To keep students engaged, I asked them to vote on the correct answer. I also staged minidebates. Generally, I withheld my own answers.

Despite the fact that lectures of this sort violated students' expectations — they even seemed to inject such alien qualities as personal judgment and opinion into the case — most students became involved in solving the problems. I believe that, by doing so, they learned more mathematics than they would have by listening to me. My worst fear — that the class would somehow fall apart — did not materialize. I could innovate without catastrophic results. At the same time, I realized that my innovation was inherently limited, since I could go only so far in a lecture room to change the student role from a passive one to an active one. Furthermore, my lectures were now seen by students as separate from the "real" course, since they contradicted the values of correct procedures and correct answers expressed by all other course components: text, quiz sections, homework, and tests.

A colleague and I then undertook to extend the idea underlying this kind of class presentation by preparing materials with a minimum of exposition in which carefully linked instructions and questions forced students to work through the basic concepts and procedures of the course (Curjel, Joss, and Monk, 1972). This, in turn, required us to write exam questions that tested for understanding and to help students study for such exams by distributing sample exams in advance. When we finished this project, a psychologist who worked with us pointed out that we had created two distinct cultures within our course. The lecture periods and materials were experience-based and intuitive. In contrast, the TAs spent quiz sessions explaining what students were to learn from the material, not making them go through it. In fact, the more the TAs perceived the professor and the materials to be process-oriented, the more they took it upon themselves to give students highly compressed summaries of the results of these processes. (For a discussion of the interactions among the components of such a course, see the chapter by Finkel and Monk in this sourcebook.)

To bring the two cultures together — or, more accurately, to bring the TAs around to our point of view — we decided to hold an extensive orientation and weekly staff meetings. TAs were happy to meet with these energetic and enthusiastic faculty members, but since their only dissatisfaction with their own teaching was the result of strange educational ideas that we had brought to the course, they saw no need to reconsider their own approach. We were struck by the parallel between out students and our TAs. Students do not learn mathematics by being told about it; they need to plunge in and do mathematics. Teachers do not change their attitudes toward teaching by being told about better approaches; they need a changed teaching activity, so that they can experience their teaching in a different way.

With our next group of TAs, we began by discussing the problems involved in teaching and learning mathematics. Then, we suggested that — as an experiment — they break students in their quiz sections into four- or five-member groups to work on the course material. They could rove around and listen to one group, help another, and prod a third; but, because there were so many students in the class, the separate groups would be on their own a good deal of the time. By introducing learning groups, we proposed to solve two different problems: Students would plunge in and do mathematics, while TAs would experience their teaching in a radically different way. Four of the five TAs agreed to this approach.

The experiment proceeded smoothly for four weeks until we were swept by a wave of discontent among the TAs. We had deprived them of their rightful place in the classroom and deprived the students of the TAs' expertise. TAs had heard our suggestion that they leave their powerful posts at the front of the room as an injunction against giving answers, and they felt irresponsible. They were deeply troubled by the "wrong ideas" that were hardening into truths in student groups that they could not attend. Listening to student groups struggle with the material seemed to prove that their attentions were critically necessary. Some students made it clear that they felt abandoned, and immediately the TAs decided that these feelings were objective descriptions of fact. The students had generally done well on the midquarter exam, but this did not reassure the TAs, who interpreted the high grades that many students received as indications that "teachers really aren't necessary"; however, they said, students who failed "might have been saved by some direct teaching."

They all agreed, however, that the students worked together with new energy and motivation and that it was much more gratifying to teach in an environment in which teachers shared the responsibility for learning with students. Students generally seemed to appreciate a course in which they could be so directly engaged with the language and ideas. And, after all, they had done well on a substantial exam. The discontent of the TAs was focused on the format of the learning groups, yet none of them advocated a return to the conventional class-room format. We were experiencing the stress that always seems to accompany social change. When the time came for the TAs to decide how to handle the remainder of the quiz sections, all four decided to continue with learning groups.

Thus, after only one quarter of rocky but successful use, the idea of breaking a quiz section into groups had become a fixture of the course, as if things had always been done that way. TAs entered the experience knowing that "they do groups in this course" and that the format would require them to make adjustments in their teaching, adjustments that could be dealt with in staff meetings. Now, after nine years of use in the course, learning groups seem so unremarkable that TAs no longer discuss them at staff meetings.

Having finally achieved at least a measure of what we had set out to do—namely, get students to engage actively in the course—my colleagues and I were in a position to make changes that caused the course to fit together better as a whole. The course material has been expanded (Monk, 1981) to supply more of the exposition than the standard text provided. Since the quiz sections serve both as a center for student activity and as a basis for forming outside study groups, the lectures can serve an increased variety of teaching functions. Generally, the lecturer uses the format of "Let's do a problem together," but sometimes gives careful explanations. Friday lectures are always reserved for answers to students' written questions. The fact that TAs cannot hope to cover all the material gives them an incentive to read reports from the lecturer about what he has done. At the same time, the experience of listening to students and guiding them gives TAs an occasion to do some reporting of their own. Their daily descriptions of the confusions, insights, and moods of their classes, together with the lecture reports, form a written chronicle of each quarter—a chronicle that TAs and professors consult regularly and that they find extremely helpful.

The original view of my power to affect 350 minds was illusory, because I interpreted my power as the capacity to tell students how to do mathematics and to direct my TAs in their teaching. Slowly, I came to realize that I could have more influence both on my students and on my TAs by shaping the terms of their experiences—by having the students become more actively engaged in doing mathematics together and by having the TAs relate to the classroom in a more flexible manner. I could then have an effect on their minds through the written materials that I provided as grist for these experiences. The prospect of

12

lecturing to a hushed roomful of students busily taking notes had seemed so momentous, yet lecturing alone had little real effect. At first, the suggestion that my TAs should break their classes into learning groups seemed innocuous enough, yet it caused a great initial uproar. Finally, however, it proves to have had an enormous influence both on the students' learning and on the course culture.

References

Curjel, C. R., Joss, R. R., and Monk, G. S. *From Problems to Calculus*. Seattle: Associated Students of the University of Washington Lecture Notes, 1972.

Monk, G. S. *Calculus in Business and Economics*. Seattle: Associated Students of the University of Washington Lecture Notes, 1981.

G. Stephen Monk is an associate professor of mathematics at the University of Washington. Cofounder, with Don Finkel, of the Evergreen Summer Institute for College Teachers, he has worked extensively with teachers from diverse disciplines to change their teaching.

Contrary to popular opinion, large classes can be productive and satisfying both for students and for teachers, but this will not happen unless students are actively involved in the learning process.

Team Learning in Large Classes

Larry K. Michaelsen

Although large classes generally reduce instructional costs, they often provoke a negative chain reaction among students and teachers. Students are forced to be passive; this produces apathy, absenteeism, and poor performance. Instructors often blame themselves, not the class structure, and search for ways to improve their delivery skills in order to recapture students' interest. When these efforts fail, instructors blame unappreciative and irresponsible students. The budding conflict can escalate if instructors use grades to force students into at least a minimum level of activity. Unfortunately, this cycle often ends in a sort of armed truce that satisfies neither side.

Team learning is an instructional format that breaks this destructive cycle through extensive use in the classroom of permanent, heterogeneous, six- or seven-member student learning groups. Team learning involves students actively in the learning process. Consistently, it has produced high levels of attendance, performance, and satisfaction in classes of as many as 180 students for a wide range of subject matters in the physical and social sciences. The work of team learning groups is the central focus of class activity, not a temporary supplement to lec-

C. Bouton and R. Y. Garth (Eds.). *Learning in Groups.* New Directions for
Teaching and Learning, no. 14. San Francisco: Jossey-Bass, June 1983.

14

tures or laboratory sessions. Consequently, the teams can harness group forces in ways that short-term groups cannot. Indeed, permanent groups become cohesive enough to serve as a major source of motivation and social support. As a result, attendance in team learning classes is exceptionally high, and the percentage of students who drop out is often quite low. Finally, the heterogeneity of team learning groups magnifies their benefits in the cognitive domain by providing a variety of approaches and viewpoints that is very useful in problem-solving discussions (Goldman, 1965).

Forming Groups

The team learning process is most effective when groups contain members with a wide variety of viewpoints and at least one member with the specific skills required for completion of assigned tasks. For example, in a physical chemistry course, every group should contain both chemistry and engineering majors. Since pre-existing friendships between individual members can impede the development of group cohesiveness, instructors should form the team learning groups themselves, relying on an inventory of students' backgrounds and competencies to identify an appropriate skills mix, and assign students to groups. One method frequently used to accomplish this task asks students to respond (either aloud or by raising their hands) to a series of questions about their backgrounds. Then, when the scarcest "resource" is known, students can stand up to be counted off into groups. Some instructors prefer to use a written questionnaire to collect the background information; these instructors sort students into groups between the first and second class meetings.

Building and Maintaining Group Cohesiveness

A major problem in the use of permanent classroom groups is providing mechanisms to ensure that groups function effectively. Unfortunately, neither of the most common strategies for building and maintaining the cohesiveness of classroom groups is practical in a large class. This is because neither training students to manage the group and solve problems that arise (Bouton, 1980) nor personal guidance by the instructor is possible with more than a handful of groups. Consequently, instructors of large classes must usually rely on someone else to build and maintain group cohesiveness, such as paid assistants, students who receive course credit (Bradford and LeDuc, 1975), or class members who have been "promoted" to "supervisory" positions by the instructor (Cohen, 1976).

Teachers can also establish external conditions that make significant intragroup conflicts unlikely. These conditions include forming groups whose heterogeneity minimizes the probability that previously established relationships will lead to counterproductive subgroups, allowing students to determine the degree to which group performance contributes to their grade (Michaelsen, Craig, and Watson, 1981), and making heavy demands and fostering competition among groups, both of which build and maintain group cohesiveness for the duration of the semester.

Sequencing Instructional Activities

Most group-oriented instructional approaches follow the traditional instructional activity sequence of lecture and individual study, followed by application (for example, cases, projects, simulations), followed by an exam. In the traditional sequence, exams provide little insight into the concepts that need to be covered in class (Bloom, Hastings, and Madaus, 1971). In addition, students often put off studying until just before an exam; as a result, they are a liability to their groups during application-oriented activities.

In team learning, the primary instructional activity is different: Individual study is followed by individual exam, group discussion and exam, lecture, and finally application (Michaelsen, Watson, and Fink, 1982). This sequence enhances learning in a number of ways. First, it places primary responsibility for learning the material on individual students in individual study, then on the group and the instructor. Second, students receive immediate feedback on how well they have learned through scoring of individual exams and discussion during the group exam. Third, the sequence provides a forum for peer teaching through discussion during the group exam and later application-oriented activities, projects, and exams. Fourth, it provides the instructor with specific information on concepts about which additional information is needed, and reduces the coverage of material that students already understand—a benefit for students and instructor alike. Fifth, it provides groups with information about each individual's level of preparation, which facilitates the development of performance-oriented group norms. Sixth, it shows students and the instructor that groups can teach their members. Group scores on exams average more than 90 percent, and they are above their highest individual member in more than 95 percent of the groups. Finally, it ensures that students will develop a working familiarity with course concepts before application-oriented activities, projects, and exams.

Organizing the Material

Since testing precedes lectures in the team learning instructional activity sequence, teachers may have to make as many as three modifications in the organization of the material that they are teaching. First, topics must be sequenced so that each provides a conceptual foundation for the next. Second, tests must be devised that allow the instructor to detect and correct misunderstandings before the next topic in the sequence is introduced. Third, the material must be divided into relatively small units, so that teachers can correct misunderstandings before students experience difficulty comprehending new material or compound previous misunderstandings with misinterpretations of additional material (Bloom, Hastings, and Madaus, 1971). Preparing for minitests constitutes the most time-consuming change, since the exams are frequent; since they are given at the beginning, not the end, of major units of instruction; and since they are the instructor's primary means for assuring that students have developed an understanding of course concepts. Instructors can often reduce the time and effort required for sequencing of topics by selecting a well-designed text and dividing the course outline into smaller units.

Developing and Managing Group-Oriented Classroom Activities

One of the unique features of team learning is that it usually enables students to become acquainted with basic terminology and concepts in less than 25 percent of class time devoted to individual and group exams and to instructor explanation of homework. As a result, instructors may develop activities for the bulk of class time that are appropriate for group work and that focus on concept applications.

Ideally, each application used in the team learning process should permit the instructor to provide feedback to students on their understanding of course concepts, provide an opportunity for peer teaching, and build group cohesiveness. Activities that have been successfully adapted for the team learning process include tests, problems, case analyses, and role plays.

However, the type of activity has much less to do with the success with which it can be used in the team learning process than two other characteristics do. First, to be effective, any group task must be carefully structured, so that students understand the kind of "product" the group is to produce, and sufficiently challenging for information from a majority of group members to be required. Studies have found that groups are more effective than individuals in solving problems that require either the pooling of information or the application of concepts that have been mastered in the abstract (Goldman, 1965; Laughlin and Johnson, 1966). Thus, when tests are given to groups, the teacher should specify the form in which answers are to be given, and the questions asked should be difficult enough that they are likely to be missed by students working alone but to be answered correctly by a group after discussion.

Many application-oriented activities, including minitests and experiential exercises, require written materials to be distributed at a certain point. Without careful planning, the time required in large classes to distribute materials or collect assignments can be prohibitive. To solve this problem, a teacher can use manila folders containing the materials that each group will need on any given day. These folders can be placed in a portable filing bucket at the front of the room. Groups can pick up their folders at the beginning of class. The instructor can control the distribution of materials by stating that the material in the folders should not be passed out until he or she says so.

A similar method can be used to collect materials. For example, the teacher can establish the rule that individual assignments must be placed in a designated folder. Thus, all materials are received in a standard-sized, clearly labeled form. The total number of items that have to be kept track of coincides with the number of groups in the class, not with the number of individuals. The folders can also provide an effective means of controlling materials. For example, if a check of folders indicates that six exams were handed out to a particular project team and that only five exams were turned in, the group can be informed of the shortage and asked to find the missing test. (Groups always do.)

Another problem posed by use of group activities in a large class is pacing. Groups have to be paced so that the teacher can work with the class as a whole. Three methods can help the instructor to coordinate the groups' work. The first method reduces the need for communication between groups by having each group produce materials that can be shared with the whole class. For example, if the class is working on an engineering problem, groups can write their key assumptions, givens, unknowns, and answers on large sheets of newsprint, which can be taped to a wall so that they are visible to the rest of the class (Michaelsen, Watson, Cragin, and Fink, 1982). The second method for reducing coordination and pacing problems schedules some group activities near the end of the class; students can leave when they complete their work. Finally, the so-called five-five rule can be used for other activities, including minitests: When five groups (25 percent of the class) have completed the activity, the remaining groups have five more minutes in which to turn in their answer sheets or other assigned work. This procedure has a bonus: It stimulates intergroup competition.

The Classroom and Schedule

Team learning requires a room in which group work can be done in reasonable comfort and in which students' group affiliations are easy to identify. The ideal classroom permits seating in a circle or at a large table. Less desirable but still workable is a tiered amphitheater: Students in adjacent rows can talk with other students by standing or turning.

Team learning works better in larger classes that meet for at least seventy-five minutes. Problem-solving discussions take a while to become productive, particularly when they are intended to develop analysis and synthesis skills (Bloom, 1956).

The Grading System

A major factor in the success of the team learning process is students' views of the relationship between their efforts and the grades that they receive. Consequently, the grading system must reinforce the type of student commitment that is required for effective problem solving. Incentives for individual preparation are needed because group productivity is likely to be low and the potential for conflict among group members is high when only one or two students are prepared.

Incentives for promoting group performance and for maintaining group cohesiveness are needed to develop a setting in which peer teaching can occur. A grading system in which group performance "counts" both legitimizes and stimulates the expenditure of effort on group tasks. Similarly, having grades based in part on students' responsiveness to one another minimizes the possibility that students will slide by on the efforts of others.

Providing Feedback and Handling Student Challenges

The team learning process depends on students' receiving feedback about group members' attendance and individual preparation and on their understanding of course concepts. The first type of feedback is essential to the development, maintenance, and enforcement of peergroup norms. It can be provided by having students record their own scores and attendance in the manila folder used to distribute and collect material (Michaelsen, Watson, Cragin, and Fink, 1982). The second type of feedback is essential to learning. It requires careful planning and attention.

Students in team learning classes develop a social support base in their groups. As a result, they are much more willing than other students are to disagree with an instructor. Although such challenges provide valuable feedback to the instructor, they can become a major problem in large classes if they disrupt the flow of activity for the entire class. Students' willingness to disagree can be a problem in providing feedback, especially on group exams. Although the groups are usually accurate in their work, the emotional commitment to incorrect answers can be very high. Allowing groups to let off steam until they are willing to consider alternatives can be both threatening and time-consuming.

There are two methods for handling disagreements while giving feedback on group tests. For preinstructional exams, groups can prepare written appeals on questions that they miss. If an appeal is accepted, it can also apply to the individual exams. This helps in several ways. First, in the process of reviewing assigned readings to prepare an appeal, students often discover that they, not the instructor, were mistaken. Second, writing the appeal reduces the need to let off steam. Third, the students and the instructor can respond more rationally, since the actual decision on the appeal is delayed until a later time. Finally, the appeals can be used to improve the questions themselves.

With essay exams, the teacher can provide feedback by temporarily reforming the groups to discuss an "ideal" answer provided by the instructor — either a reproduction of the best answer obtained from groups in the class or a composite of the best answers. In most cases, discussions within groups can resolve misunderstandings, since the majority of group members usually understand the "ideal" answer. As a result, confrontations seldom occur, and later class discussions focus on additional perspectives.

Results of Team Learning in Large Classes

Results from use of team learning in large (120-plus students) undergraduate classes in organizational behavior at the University of Oklahoma suggest that students can be extremely successful in understanding conceptual material. Scores on identical true-and-false, multiple-choice minitests have been virtually the same in large undergraduate classes and in twenty- to thirty-member graduate classes. Student evaluations of their own progress on learning fundamental principles, generalizations, and theories have consistently been around the ninetieth percentile on the IDEA evaluation instrument marketed by the Center for Faculty Evaluation and Development, Kansas State University. Student performance on exams treating complex case material (for example, novels and full-length feature films) has been of consistently high quality. Students' ratings of their own progress in improvement of thinking and problem-solving skills in large team learning classes have been consistently well above the ninetieth percentile on the IDEA scale.

Other evidence of the effectiveness of the team learning process in large classes includes very positive attitudes toward the course. Although the amount of reading and other work required for the course has been rated above the ninetieth percentile, compared to other courses on the IDEA scale, students also rate the team learning course as one of the top two courses in the college of business. Furthermore, when students are asked to indicate how the size of the class affected what they gained from taking the course, an average of 50 percent maintains that the large size actually "helped more than it hurt." Only 8 percent indicated that the large class size "hurt more than it helped." Student ratings of the extent to which the course resulted in "more positive feelings toward this field of study" have been above the ninetieth percentile, according to IDEA norms.

Ninety-nine percent of the students who have signed up for the class have maintained their enrollment throughout the semester, and 97 percent were present every time that the class met, although there were no penalties for absence. Approximately 65 percent of the students identify either "feelings of responsibility for" or "expectations of" the group as being the most important factor in their attendance at class. Other factors included "interesting class" (5 percent), "instructor expectations" (2 percent), and "grades" (28 percent).

Team learning has produced a number of other desirable outcomes in a variety of physical and social science courses. Many of these outcomes result from the intensive interaction required in teams and from the incentive system designed to encourage students to support one another and to contribute to the work of the group. Students who are well prepared in subject matter are rewarded through peer evaluation, because they help other team members to acquire basic skills. At the same time, they develop their own teaching skills. Older students returning to school are rewarded, because they provide a realistic perspective on the problems to be solved, and because they gain confidence in their ability to work and compete with younger students. Students with experience in other cultures expand the horizons of discussions. Moreover, the team learning process gives students experience in working in groups. This experience can help them later in work settings, where group problem solving is important to success.

In sum, students benefit from team learning in important ways: They are actively involved in the learning process, they receive immediate feedback, they have ready access to individual help, and they have an opportunity to work on challenging problems. Other benefits extend beyond the classroom: Team learning groups foster friendship and social support, they provide information about coping with the demands of the university bureaucracy, and they give students an opportunity to develop interpersonal and group skills.

The use of team learning also enriches the experience for instructors. Since students learn most of the basic concepts either on their own or from peers, the instructor receives fewer requests for individual help, but the requests that do occur are more challenging and rewarding. In addition, the team learning process so increases the frequency and candor of student feedback that, even in large classes, teaching is a very personal experience. Finally, the team learning process allows instructors to meet demands to teach larger classes without feeling guilty about the learning that takes place there.

References

Bloom, B. S. *Taxonomy of Educational Objectives: The Classification of Educational Goals.* New York: McKay, 1956.

Bloom, B. S., Hastings, J. T., and Madaus, B. F. *Handbook on Formative and Summative Evaluation of Student Learning.* New York: McGraw-Hill, 1971.

Bouton, C. *The Cooperative Learning Project Student Manual.* Washington: University of the District of Columbia, 1980.

Bradford, D., and LeDuc, R. "One Approach to the Core and Teaching of Introductory Organizational Behavior." *Exchange: The Organizational Behavior Teaching Journal,* 1975, *1* (1), 23-30.

Cohen, A. R. "Beyond Simulation: Treating the Classroom as an Organization." *Exchange: The Organizational Behavior Teaching Journal,* 1976, *2* (1), 13-18.

Goldman, M. "A Comparison of Individual and Group Performance for Varying Combinations of Individual Ability." *Journal of Personality and Social Psychology,* 1965, *1,* 210-216.

Laughlin, P., and Johnson, H. "Group and Individual Performance on a Complementary Task as a Function of Initial Ability Level." *Journal of Experimental Social Psychology,* 1966, *2,* 407-414.

Michaelsen, L. K., Cragin, J. P., and Watson, W. E. "Grading and Anxiety: A Strategy for Coping." *Exchange: The Organizational Behavior Teaching Journal,* 1981, *6* (1), 8-14.

Michaelsen, L. K., Watson, W. E., and Fink, L. D. "Mini Tests: A Practical Approach to Mastery Learning." Unpublished manuscript, University of Oklahoma, 1982.

Michaelsen, L. K., Watson, W. E., Cragin, J. P., and Fink, L. D. "Team Learning: A Potential Solution to the Problems of Large Classes." *Exchange: The Organizational Behavior Teaching Journal,* 1982, *7* (1), 13-22.

Larry K. Michaelsen, associate professor of management at the University of Oklahoma, serves on the editorial board of Exchange: The Organizational Behavior Teaching Journal. *He has worked extensively with teachers on the use of classroom learning groups, and he pioneered the development of team learning, a group-centered teaching format now being used in Australia, China, and the U.S. in a wide variety of physical science, social science, and humanities courses.*

Collaboration bridges the gap between the solitary act
of writing and the conversation of which it is part.

Teaching Writing
Through Collaboration

Kenneth A. Bruffee

The phrase *writing crisis* is familiar to almost everyone by now. It reminds us that all is not entirely well in the groves of academe — at least since the phrase became current in the early 1970s. The quality of undergraduate writing became a national issue when the popular press discovered that large and apparently increasing numbers of college graduates had difficulty expressing themselves cogently or even grammatically in writing.

The true extent and nature of the writing crisis was not clear at first, however, because the beginning of public interest in student writing coincided with the beginning of open admissions programs at such large and conspicuous institutions as the City University of New York. As a result of this coincidence, the general public, along with many university faculty members and administrators throughout the country, became persuaded that the students who wrote poorly must be some of the poorly prepared new students who perhaps did not belong in college at all.

This perception of the writing crisis began to change only in the mid 1970s, when rumors spread that concerned faculty members at

C. Bouton and R. Y. Garth (Eds.). *Learning in Groups.* New Directions for
Teaching and Learning, no. 14. San Francisco: Jossey-Bass, June 1983.

several Ivy League universities had met privately to consider the writing crisis among their own highly select students. When the profession learned that a major international banking firm was trying to hire someone to teach its Harvard M.B.A.s to write memos that would not mire industrial progress in conceptual incoherence and syntactical confusion, the cat was out of the bag. The writing crisis was not confined to nontraditional students. Indeed, if the quality of writing in government publications and professional journals could be taken as evidence, the writing crisis was not even particularly new. It involved many well-educated, competent people, and it was at least a generation old. Writing well seemed to be as difficult for many university teachers as it was for their students.

For a time, blame for the writing crisis was widely and eagerly placed. And, for a time, solutions proliferated. By the late 1970s, dozens of ways to solve every writing problem had been proposed, although little more than anecdotal evidence was provided that they could work. This situation began to change with the publication of Mina Shaughnessy's (1977) elegant, scholarly study of inept writing, *Errors and Expectations.* Shaughnessy's book gave us both a reasoned analysis of what we mean by *poor writing* and a survey of what then seemed to be the most effective ways of dealing with it.

Writing as a Collaborative or Social Activity: Brooklyn College

Most of the approaches to the teaching of writing that Shaughnessy surveyed have at least one thing in common: Most assume that writing, like reading, is an individual activity done in private. Experienced readers assume that there was once an author, somewhere, who wrote what they read. Experienced writers assume that someone, somewhere, may read what they write. But, many inexperienced writers feel isolated when they write, like castaways on a desert island. What they write, they tend to feel, is little more than a note in a bottle afloat on a solitary sea. The writing has no known destination, no hope of a reader who might be called a friend. Certainly, most of us perform the act of reading or writing alone. As a result, many people today feel a reluctance to write, because writing seems to cut us off from the experience of direct relations with our peers. Of course, student writers do know that one person — the teacher — will read what they write. But, they take little comfort in knowing that this person will not read primarily to understand, sympathize, or respond to what they say but to judge how they say it.

The long-term effect of this experience of both writing and reading as solitary acts is that we fail to see that reading and writing are private, individual activities only on the surface. In reality, both reading and writing are social acts that we displace into privacy for convenience. Writing in particular is social in nature. It is so because writing is externalized thought, and thought itself is internalized social and public conversation (Bruffee, 1980b). Writing is, therefore, not an individual act but an individualized act. To begin at the beginning with writing is to begin with the community that maintains the sort of conversation out of which writing is generated.

Of the many ways of dealing with poor student writing that Shaughnessy mentions, at least one (Shaughnessy, 1977, p. 83) is based on this principle — a small program at Brooklyn College that organizes undergraduates to tutor each other in writing. The success of this program is demonstrated by the fact that, during its early years, in which Brooklyn College experienced abnormal growth, the program logged some 1,000 hours of tutoring each semester. More recently, after the college had shrunk to half its former size, the peer tutoring program shrank proportionately. But, throughout the merciless budget cutting at City University of New York in the late 1970s, the college never abandoned peer tutoring. The program celebrated its tenth anniversary in spring 1983. In 1976, it received a national award for excellence as a pedagogical innovation. And, it spawned a program of federally funded summer institutes in which teachers from across the nation have been trained to teach tutors as tutors are taught in the Brooklyn College program. Some two dozen such programs have been established at postsecondary institutions across the country.

The success of the program can be attributed in part to the fact that it benefits both peer tutors and tutees. Tutees get help when they need it — on a drop-in basis and under conditions that are conducive to good writing. There is no red tape, the atmosphere is unhurried, and they are in the company not of evaluating faculty but of sympathetic fellow students. Peer tutors benefit from the opportunity to serve both their classmates and the college at large in an important way. Further, the program contributes to the liberal education of peer tutors by providing a context both for their personal and intellectual development and for their development as writers (Bruffee, 1978).

The success of the program can also be attributed in part to the fact that, both in the tutoring process and in the training of tutors, writing is assumed to be a social activity. Peer tutoring is a collaborative activity in which tutor and tutee work together in a two-member learning group. Tutors can learn as much from tutees and from tutoring as tutees can learn from tutors. To ensure that peer tutoring becomes a two-way street, tutors are trained in a credit-bearing course in advanced composition taught almost exclusively with learning groups. Bruffee (1980a) describes the syllabus of this course, details many of the learning group problems posed to peer tutors, and explains how learning groups and other kinds of collaborative learning procedures can be used in teaching introductory expository writing courses.

In the tutor-training course, peer tutors work with each other in a way analogous to that in which they tutor students in the tutoring program. Tutors write short essays, then use the essays as raw material in learning to write progressively more complex, demanding, and tactfully helpful critiques of each other's work. Thus, the course is designed to make each step in the displaced social process of writing directly social again, so that the writing process can be refined in collaboration with others and then, in effect, reinternalized. Tutors practice each step in learning groups. Usually, these groups have five or six members. Sometimes, they have only two; other times, the group is the whole class. By working through such problems as defining topics, gaining focus, establishing unity and coherence, and writing effective introductions in learning groups, students learn how to solve many of their own writing problems as well as those of the students whom they will help.

The normal way in which learning groups are used in the course is itself of interest, because it is a model that can be transferred with profit to courses in other fields of study. At the beginning of the class hour, the teacher organizes the students into groups and poses a problem or task. Each group then appoints a recorder, who takes notes on the group's discussion and reports the results to the rest of the class. Each group should reach a consensus in its discussion—not unanimity but a decision that everyone in the group can live with. Dissent is encouraged, although it is not provoked, and it is reported as an addendum to each group's consensual decision.

The plenary session that follows the small-group discussions begins with the recorder's reports. The teacher acts as moderator, helping the class as a whole to work toward a consensus among groups. New ideas often emerge at this point, as people hear the reports of other groups. Dissent is encouraged, too, and it often happens that dissent in one group matches the consensus reached by another. In any case, dissent can open the door to fruitful free-for-all debate. The goal of this phase of the process is for the class as a whole either to reach a consensus based on the discussions in small groups or to acknowledge and fully articulate an agreement to disagree.

Now, the teacher's role again changes. In the new role, the teacher serves as a representative of the larger community of competent writers and readers or of the community of liberally educated adults. In this role, the teacher compares the current consensus of the larger community with the consensus reached by the class. If the class consensus seems to agree with the consensus of the larger community, the discussion on this point ends for the moment. If the class consensus does not agree with the consensus of the larger community, then the discussion enters another phase. Here, the question is not, Who is right? but, How do the processes by which the class and the larger community arrived at their consensus differ? That is, the last issue that is discussed in a learning group class of this sort can be — and often is — the elements of consensual conversation itself.

The purpose of this last phase of discussion is to help students understand how knowledge communities deal with dissent; that is, how consensus in a knowledge community changes. Thus, a course taught in this way holds enormous potential for students' intellectual growth. The process engages students' interest at the immediate, concrete level on which the problem is presented initially. It involves them in discussion on points of substance and judgment integral with the field of study in question. Finally, it can raise their conceptual awareness of issues in the field to a level of considerable sophistication. The process can do all this largely without direct intervention by the teacher as a purveyor of information or doctrine. The teacher's role is neither that of performer, nor oracle, nor facilitator. The teacher sets tasks that students undertake collaboratively: to write, to examine writing formally, and to evaluate writing. As such, the teacher is a representative of the community of literate, knowledgeable people appointed to help students to become full members of that community.

Acknowledged Collaboration: Beaver College

Teachers at Beaver College play a similar role in students' learning to write. However, at Beaver, not all the teachers in question are professional teachers of writing. They are teachers in many fields. The writing-across-the-curriculum program established by Elaine Maimon and her colleagues during the early 1970s is a model of academic collegiality. There, the emphasis is on the process that precedes the moment when writers go public with their writing.

Teachers in all fields are counseled to create contexts in which students read each other's work in progress. These contexts often involve formal group work in classes; even more often, they involve informal work in groups outside class. In this work, students hear their own and each other's writing voice. They learn, for themselves as well as for others, that the tone of voice that puts writers on the defensive defeats writing. They learn that they themselves often hear voices of this sort and that they put themselves on the defensive as writers. Students working in writing groups are taught instead to ask where their peers are coming from as the author of a given essay and where they hope to go with the piece. Thus, writing groups, whether formal or informal, help students to learn how writers behave and to become helpful and productive members of the community of effective writers.

The Beaver program is built on the assumption — made in most fields of academic study — that research is not complete until it has been reported; that is, until it has been offered to a community of knowledgeable peers for response. Thus, writing groups are really rewriting groups, in which students find out, many for the first time, that rewriting is not punishment for doing badly the first time but an opportunity to offer one's best work to the community that counts. Students are required to acknowledge all this collaborative work on an acknowledgments page that accompanies every essay made public. Acknowledgment does more than ensure every student and teacher against plagiarism. It teaches the difference between debt and documentation and it connects every writer with the community of peers.

Like the Brooklyn College program, the success of the Beaver College program can be measured by its longevity: more than five years in full force. It can also be measured by its power to engage more than half the full-time faculty of the college in active work to improve student writing. Finally, its success can be measured by the federally funded workshops that have, over the years, introduced dozens of faculty members from colleges and high schools across the country to its procedures. A textbook for programs of this type (Maimon and others, 1981) provides instructions for teachers in a variety of fields.

Summary

Together, the Brooklyn College and Beaver College programs seem to show that peer-group influence has great educative potential in the teaching of writing. Both programs assume that the causes of the writing crisis are more complex than poor preparation. Both offer relatively simple ways of adjusting the social context of learning so as both to democratize it and at the same time to maintain, perhaps in some cases even to increase, rigor. Finally, both return students from the alienation of private and isolated study to what Oakeshott (1980) has called the "conversation of mankind."

References

Bruffee, K. A. "The Brooklyn Plan: Attaining Intellectual Growth through Peer-Group Tutoring." *Liberal Education,* 1978, *64,* 447–468.

Bruffee, K. A. *A Short Course in Writing.* (2nd ed.) Cambridge, Mass.: Winthrop, 1980a.

Bruffee, K. A. "Writing and Reading as Collaborative or Social Acts: The Argument from Kuhn and Vygotsky." Paper presented at the Skidmore Conference on Writing and Thought, 1980b.

Maimon, E., and others. *Writing in the Arts and Sciences.* Cambridge, Mass.: Winthrop, 1981.

Oakeshott, M. "The Voice of Poetry in the Conversation of Mankind." In M. Oakeshott (Ed.), *Rationalism in Politics.* New York: Basic Books, 1962.

Shaughnessy, M. P. *Errors and Expectations.* New York: Oxford University Press, 1977.

Kenneth A. Bruffee is a professor in the Department of English at Brooklyn College, City of New York. For several years, he has conducted a summer workshop to help college faculty from all over the country establish programs of collaborative learning through peer tutoring.

Teachers do not have to choose between emphasizing course content and developing students skills. Both are integral parts of a cooperative learning process.

Developing Student Skills and Abilities

Clark Bouton
Beryl Rice

During the past decade, there have been increasing complaints about the low level of skills and abilities that college students possess. Complaints range from specific skills, such as writing, to broad abilities, such as reasoning and problem solving. The complaints have focused on skills that students need in order to succeed in traditional college classes. However, the skills problem appears to be far more serious when one notes that the skills that students do acquire in college seem to have little relevance to the skills needed outside the classroom. Research shows that the best students do no better than other students in terms of significant achievement or career success (Hoyt, 1966; Hudson, 1960). Such research has elicited surprisingly little response from the academic community, but it suggests that traditional teaching methods develop neither academic skills nor the skills necessary for success outside college.

The prevalent response to students' deficiencies in academic skills has been to demand more skills courses. For their part, teachers

C. Bouton and R. Y. Garth (Eds.). *Learning in Groups.* New Directions for Teaching and Learning, no. 14. San Francisco: Jossey-Bass, June 1983.

attempt to get the content of their courses across to students in ways that reduce the demands on students' skills. This response is self-defeating. Skills do not exist in the abstract, and students cannot learn a skill, such as writing, much less thinking, in one or two skills courses. However, both by avoiding their share of the responsibility for developing students' skills and by using teaching methods that attempt to compensate for students' low level of skills, teachers deprive students of the chance to develop needed skills. Given the training that college teachers receive and the fragmentation of curriculum into specialized subject matters, the teacher is primarily concerned with covering the material of a course, and the development of skills seems to belong either to other specialists or to no one in particular.

The Cooperative Learning Project

The Cooperative Learning Project at the University of the District of Columbia grew out of the conviction that content and skills cannot be separated; both are part of a single learning process. Knowledge that goes beyond mere information is always knowledge of how to do something, and skills can only be developed by use. The goal of the project has been to develop a teaching method that actively engages students in a learning process that enables them both to acquire a knowledge of the material and to develop their skills in the process of acquiring that knowledge. The success of the project and the results of others' experience with learning groups indicate that that goal can be achieved.

The University of the District of Columbia is a public institution; it has low tuition, an open-door admissions policy, and a predominantly black enrollment. The students are typically nontraditional in that they commute to school, they are older than the average college student, their parents lack college degrees, and, in many cases, they are enrolled part-time. The skills deficiencies of these students may be more severe than, but not different in kind from, those of other college students. While some students need special courses on specific skills, all students need continuous practice to develop the skills and abilities not provided by traditional teaching methods.

The project has trained 40 teachers in disciplines across the curriculum to use student learning groups in place of the traditional lecture-discussion method of teaching. The way in which the project uses groups differs significantly from the typical way in which groups are used in college classes. Specific features of the project method and their rationale can be described under five headings.

Classes are Group-Centered. Group activity is central, not supplementary, in project classes. Lecture and teacher-led discussion are virtually eliminated. We have found that the information and guidance provided by traditional methods can be provided more effectively in other ways. More important, the student's passive and dependent role and the teacher's role of responsible authority and focus of attention are too deeply ingrained to be changed by anything less than a radical alteration in the interaction between them. Sufficient time to adapt to new roles is another requisite.

Teachers Receive Training. Teachers attend a two-week full-time training workshop before they begin teaching in the project. They also participate in an instructional work group during the first semester. The training workshop teaches participants to work with groups and to design learning plans, and it provides actual teaching experience with student learning groups. Teachers need training and experience to work effectively with groups. In the workshop and work group, teachers are given the training and support that they need. Training includes a review of the literature on group process. Most important, the training group analyzes its own interactions. Teachers tend to think in terms of how to tell students what they want them to know. Therefore, most trainees experience great difficulty at first in designing activities that enable students to learn independently. The work groups provide teachers with mutual support and assistance during the difficult period when the method is first being used.

Group Activities Are Structured. Classroom group activities are highly structured, with explicit goals and activities. Students whose entire educational experience has been in traditional classrooms do not do well when suddenly left to their own resources in self-led groups. Therefore, group learning activities in project classes are specified by the instructor at first. As student groups learn to function effectively, they are given progressively more autonomy. The goal is for groups to acquire the ability to develop their own learning plans, using the teacher as a resource and consultant.

The instructor designs a detailed learning plan for each class session or for a single topic that requires several sessions. The plan specifies learning goals, which include both the course content to be covered and the skills to be developed; activities that will enable students to achieve learning goals; a schedule that assigns specific time for each part of the learning plan; evaluation, which enables both students and teacher to assess the learning; and review of the learning plan itself, in order to determine what worked, what did not, and what subsequent plans will need. Within this basic format, there is no typical plan. The strength of the method is that it enables the individual teacher to respond to the needs of the particular class. Plans can focus on learning facts, practicing a skill, understanding a concept, or strengthening group interaction. Teachers can become very creative and provide students with varied and interesting experiences.

Designing the plan forces teachers to decide what students should learn, how much time is available, what students need and can do, what the sequence of learning should be, and what difficulties can be encountered. Content, skills, and evaluation are integral parts of the learning process. Learning is not the passive absorption of content. Learning comes with the active use of content—analyzing, inferring, relating, applying, and so forth. The learning activity focuses attention equally on skills and content, from basic reading, writing, speaking, and listening to reasoning and problem solving. Prompt evaluation by students and teachers alike provides continuous information and reinforcement to guide the course of learning. The method encourages students to become conscious of their own process of learning and prepares them to become independent learners.

Groups are Long-Term. Students usually work together in the same group for an entire semester. It takes time for each group to become a cohesive, effective unit. It also takes time to establish the conditions for learning—a willingness to take risks, to accept correction, and to respond to others critically. Long-term groups make personal and complex interactions between members possible; while this presents some difficulties, it also enables a level of learning to be reached that is not possible in short-term groups.

Goals Include Development of Abilities and Attitudes. The development of new attitudes and abilities is an important goal of the method. At the beginning of a semester, the teacher explains that the method will place new responsibilities on the student and require them to learn new behavior. Students work consciously to improve their performance in the group; in the process, they acquire abilities that are just as important outside the classroom.

The project operates with the usual framework of class periods, course descriptions, and student enrollments. Teachers who participate in the project teach their regular courses. In many cases, students register for a project course without knowing that the learning group method will be used. This has enabled us to compare the group learning method with the traditional method under equal conditions.

Evaluations by Students and Teachers

The experience of students and teachers in project classes has been ascertained through interviews, questionnaires, class observations, and discussions. All these sources provide a consistently favorable assessment and reveal significant agreement between students and teachers.

Student evaluations of the effectiveness of group learning can be seen in their answers to questions related to the project's main objectives. Students were asked to compare the learning group method to traditional teaching methods using a scale of one to five: one rates the learning group method as much worse than the traditional method, and five rates it as much better. The average rating of teaching effectiveness was 3.93; of course content learned, 4.1; of enjoyment of the class, 4.1; and of developing learning skills, 4.15.

These scores show that students responded well to the learning group method. Indeed, they rated it superior to the traditional method in teaching effectiveness, skills development, content learning, and enjoyment. Here are some typical comments: "I feel better and know more." "It gave me a sense of being independent." "It increased my studying of material." "I am less afraid of people; I study, think, and express myself better." "I feel I am developing skills essential in the real world of work." "I feel I retained a lot more information than in the lecture method." "Compared to the traditional course, this was more stimulating, interesting, and rewarding." "I like the group method, because you have to work." Of course, there were also some critical comments. Such comments expressed concern that some students were less prepared than others; thus, they did not contribute much to the group. Other critical comments indicated that some students were unwilling to change what had been successful for them.

While the majority of students expressed a preference for the learning group method in subsequent courses, the actual number of these students is less than one might expect, considering their very positive response to other questions regarding the method. Moreover, some students who rated the method as superior on all counts failed to express a preference for it in other courses. This ambivalence is revealing. While students say that they get much more from the group method than from the traditional method, they also say that they put much more work into it, and they show some reluctance to put forth equivalent effort in all their classes. It is hard for students to give up the notion that knowledge can somehow be "given" to them.

Teacher evaluations of the learning group method closely match those of students. On a questionnaire that asked them to evaluate the improvement in student performance using a five-point scale on which one indicated no improvement over the traditional method and five indicated much improvement, these were the average responses:

Student acceptance of the method	3.6
Dropouts	3.7
Absences	3.6
Student participation	4.4
Student preparation for class	4.0
Learning of course content	3.8
Development of skills	4.1
Reading comprehension	3.6
Writing	4.1
Listening and speaking	3.8
Student responsibility for learning	4.2
Awareness of the learning process	3.6
Positive student interaction	4.6
Teaching effectiveness	4.2

Thus, teachers experienced significant improvement in every aspect of student performance.

What the method has meant to teachers can best be seen in their comments on questionnaires and at workshops and meetings. There are some common themes. First, teachers note changes of behavior as students move from a passive role to an active role: "Students are more alert and alive." "There is a sense of excitement and participation—a feeling that something is going to happen today." "There is a heightened feeling of accomplishment in the students." Teachers frequently express satisfaction in the students' increased confidence, responsibility for learning, and sense of power and control.

They also note a resistance to the new method, which at one time or another many students share. Students are anxious about group work and peer relations and uncertain about their new role. Sometimes, students' past experience leads them to suspect that the teacher is not doing his job if he is not lecturing and that they are being asked to teach each other. These anxieties usually give way to favorable responses.

However, a few students cannot accept the new role. Unfortunately, these are the students who most need to develop the skills in working with others that the new method fosters.

Second, as students begin to learn cooperatively, teachers note changes in the classroom. They see "reduced learning anxiety," "a friendly learning atmosphere," "students giving each other support," and "a closeness they seldom have in traditional classes." All these changes are nicely summed up in one teacher's comment: "The groups took ownership of their own learning. The students had what is comparable to a university community. They worked outside the classroom; they called each other on the telephone; they cared about their fellow student in terms of learning and otherwise."

Of course, the increased interaction produced some conflicts between students, which neither teachers not students were experienced in handling. One teacher noted the "acrimony and bitterness that develop when students accuse one another of shirking responsibility." The cooperative method makes such behavior as absence and lack of preparation an issue between students, not just between the teacher and individual students. Peer pressure can be a powerful factor in increasing motivation, but students and teachers need to learn to deal with it. Teachers frequently note a need to improve their skills in this area.

Third, when teachers reflect on their own effectiveness, many state that one basic strength of the method is the opportunity that it gives to observe students. Teachers noted that they developed an increased sensitivity to students' needs and demands and increased flexibility to alter directions as necessary. They credited the method for providing an opportunity to "observe student growth" and a "chance to know each student." One teacher commented: "I am now able to more effectively assess how students learn; that is, how they glean information, how they evaluate what they read, and how they apply what they have learned in their own experience."

Increased knowledge about their students increased teachers' ability "to design appropriate lessons." It also made them "more confident about trying new things" and allowed for "creativity in structuring new materials." The method encourages teachers to become experimentalists. That is, they assess student needs and abilities, design an appropriate learning plan, observe students conducting the activity, evaluate the results of the activity, and review the experience with the students. As a result, teachers are always receiving prompt critical comments, which encourage them to modify their teaching and materials. It also makes teachers conscious of the need to develop a better understanding of the learning process. Teachers experiment with many variations on the method. Perhaps the central question is, What do the students need from the teacher, and what can they do for themselves? Related to this is the question of how responsibility should be shared between teacher and students.

Fourth, while it is often asserted that group learning is good only in some disciplines and some courses, the University of the District of Columbia experience shows that the method works well across disciplines and across courses. Of course, individual teachers have had varying degrees of success with the method, but these variations correlate neither with the type of discipline nor with the type or level of course. What is remarkable are the differences that a teacher encounters between two classes and between student groups in a single class. The complex interaction in group learning classes introduces new variables, and the quality of the interaction in individual student groups seems to be a major factor in determining the success of its members.

Fifth, while teachers consistently report that their participation in the project has been a rewarding experience, there are important differences in what that experience has meant. For some, the project has helped them to acquire more effective means of achieving their teaching goals. For others, it has profoundly changed their ideas of education—not only the means but the goals as well. Still others have been personally affected in their sense of self and in their relations with others.

The teachers in the project are themselves engaged in a group learning experience. Both the initial training and their continuing cooperation closely resemble what their students encounter, and their understanding of the method results in part from their own experience. What they observe in their own groups is very similar to what they see in their students.

Implications of Project Experience

What generalizations are suggested by the project's experience? First, in regard to instructional development in general, the results are encouraging. Teachers and students can assume radically different roles, for which neither their training nor their previous experience have prepared them. In particular, the learning group method seems to have three important advantages: The change in roles that it requires is significant enough to challenge individuals' assumptions about teaching and learning. Next, the opportunity that it provides to observe students learning encourages further reflection. Finally, the group method itself provides the support and assistance that encourages new learning for teachers as well as for students.

Second, our experience shows that the learning group method can be more effective than the traditional method even for teachers and students who are just learning to use it. The potential of the method could only be measured with teachers and students who have had experience in a number of learning group classes.

Third, despite assumptions that they cannot, teachers have shown that they can both involve students actively in the learning process and cover as much of the content as they would in traditional classes. Since students learn content through their own efforts, the learning should be retained longer, the level of comprehension should be higher and the learning should be more usable. Teachers and students both find it necessary to resist their tendency to focus on answers; they become able to see that an answer has little meaning until one has worked through the question and incorporated the answer into his own thought. Once this is understood, the contrast between teaching skills and teaching content is seen to rest on a false dichotomy. The most effective way to teach content is also the most effective way to develop skills.

Fourth, since students seldom have an opportunity to take more than one or two courses that use learning groups, it is impossible to assess how much more the method can improve student skills. However, despite the fact that new skills are not learned and old habits are not overcome overnight, both teachers and students see great improvement in student skills. This stands to reason; skills can only be developed by practice. In the group method, students do for themselves much of what the teacher tries to do for them with the traditional method.

Fifth, at least as important as specific academic skills is the broad range of abilities developed by the learning group method. Traditional teaching methods rarely give students the opportunity to practice abilities that are important outside the classroom; and paradoxically, precisely these abilities are often mentioned as goals of liberal education. A broad range of interpersonal, problem-solving, and communication skills are more important for successful career performance than any particular knowledge that students can acquire in college. The active involvement in the learning process and the complex interaction in cooperative learning that learning groups provide give students continual opportunities to practice these abilities. Students often report that they have made use of their newly developed abilities at work or in other activities.

Thus, learning group method offers not only a way of improving student learning of specific academic skills but also of achieving the goal of liberal education: the intellectual and social growth of students. By removing students from the role of classroom spectator and by involving them in complex interaction, the learning group method provides a superior context for the acquisition both of knowledge and of skills.

References

Hoyt, D. P. "College Grades and Adult Accomplishment: A Review of Research." *Educational Record,* 1966, *47,* 70–75.
Hudson, L. "Degree Class and Attainment in Scientific Research." *British Journal of Psychology,* 1960, *51,* 67–73.

Clark Bouton is a professor of sociology at the University of the District of Columbia. He has written, led workshops, and received grants to study the use of learning groups in college teaching.

Beryl Rice is director of the Cooperative Learning Project, associate professor in the Department of Social Welfare at the University of the District of Columbia, and teaches courses in group work and group therapy.

*Professional school education involves much more than the
teaching of facts; students must learn how to use their
knowledge in the performance of a professional role.*

Developing Professional Competence

*Larry K. Michaelsen
Scott Obenshain*

On the surface, the tasks that professionals perform and the curricula
that professional schools follow in preparing professionals seem to have
little in common. Yet, professional abilities, such as designing an effective offshore wave-measuring device, successfully treating a patient
with recurrent headaches, successfully defending someone charged
with assault on a police officer, and efficiently managing a restaurant
all require three attributes: knowledge of a set of concepts and facts
about the problem (Woods and others, 1979); an ability to combine
these concepts and facts in a holistic way, that is, an ability to solve
problems through the exercise of judgment (Nadler and Seireg, 1982);
and an ability to relate to others in the context of a professional role
(Williamson and Hudspeth, 1982).

Traditionally, classroom instruction relevant to the development of professional competence has been separated into three distinct
phases corresponding to these attributes (Flexner, 1910; Woods and
others, 1979). Unfortunately, such compartmentalization often produces problems and creates anxiety for professional school students.
During the first phase, when students typically enroll in core science or
tool courses, they often have difficulty understanding the relevance of

C. Bouton and R. Y. Garth (Eds.). *Learning in Groups.* New Directions for
Teaching and Learning, no. 14. San Francisco: Jossey-Bass, June 1983.

seemingly numberless concepts and facts that must be learned. When they enter the application phase, they enroll in courses that focus on solving problems within the various professional school disciplines. There, students have difficulty coping with the anxiety of learning how to learn. This occurs because instructors in the tool courses make most of the decisions about the facts that have to be learned. At this stage, however, it becomes essential for students to inquire, not to absorb, in order to define and solve problems (Glasser, 1969). In the last phase of their program, students often experience anxiety when they receive their first real exposure to the holistic perspective of their future professional role in the context of an integrative experience, such as a capstone course, simulation, practicum, or internship. This time, however, the anxiety can have multiple sources: open-ended problems that can only be solved by integrating concepts and facts from several disciplines, having to work closely with other professionals (Williamson and Hudspeth, 1982), and working for the first time on real problems. Table 1 summarizes these educational phases.

This chapter describes two programs — a program in medicine at the University of New Mexico and a program in business at the University of Oklahoma — in which the use of learning groups has both improved the integration of knowledge acquisition with knowledge application and encouraged the development of competencies and perspectives required to perform a professional role.

Learning Groups in Medical Education

Physicians are educated to assume the awesome responsibility associated with tremendous power. Among the most important aspects of medical education are learning to manage responsibility, acquiring adequate knowledge, and developing good communication skills. The eventual outcome — the competence of the individual physician — ultimately rests with the individual; however, the entire system of medical education has a significant impact on that outcome. Since 1910, when Abraham Flexner made his report on the state of medical education in the United States, medical education has separated the acquisition of concepts from the application of concepts.

A Quiet Revolution. In the mid 1960s, a new medical school was being planned at McMaster University in Hamilton, Ontario, Canada. Under the leadership of John Evans, the faculty set out to revamp the way in which medicine was taught. Calling on their collective experience of how physicians learn and realizing that the memory-

Table 1. Characteristics and Problems of Three Phases of Professional School Education and Partial Solutions in Two Programs That Utilize Learning Groups

	Phase One: Concept Acquisition	Phase Two: Application	Phase Three: Integration
Traditional Instructional Medium	Undergraduate or prerequisite courses and science or tool courses in early professional school	Discipline-specific professional school courses that focus on problem-solving skills	Capstone courses, simulations, practicums, internships that focus on holistic perspective and understanding of the professional role
Major Problem(s)	Understanding concepts within the larger scheme of things	Student anxiety about deficient preparation, uncertainties involved in the problem-solving process	Student anxiety created by focus on failures, complex problems, unfamiliar surroundings
Solution from Learning Groups in Primary Care Curriculum (University of New Mexico)	Acquisition of basic concepts as needed to solve problems	Considerable experience in solving problems	Considerable experience in solving problems, increased ability to locate resources, increased interpersonal skills, exposure to accurate role model
Solution from Learning Groups on Preinstructional Minitests (University of Oklahoma)	Decreased time devoted to learning concepts, increased emphasis on applications in basic courses	Previous experience with solving problems in basic courses	History of successes, previous experience in solving problems in basic courses, increased interpersonal skills

44

based approach had major failings, they designed a curriculum in which students were responsible for deciding what knowledge was needed to solve problems. The methodology adopted at McMaster was designed to assist students to learn how to learn and to become responsible for their own learning.

The McMaster teaching method emphasizes the process of group problem solving over simple recall of information. Students work in learning groups, where their task is to acquire basic science concepts and to use the scientific method as they attempt to diagnose patients' problems. These learning groups are facilitated by a tutor, whose job is to challenge the students, provide direction for novice learners, and monitor the small-group process in an effort to assure that tasks are accomplished (Hamilton, 1976; Neufeld and Barrows, 1974; Spaulding, 1969).

Building on these concepts, the University of New Mexico School of Medicine developed the primary care curriculum (PCC) (Kaufman and others, 1980). In contrast to students in traditional programs, who spend their first two years in medical school taking basic science courses, PCC students are expected to acquire the basic science concepts through small-group tutorials and self-directed study organized around a systematic series of patient problems characteristic of those found in clinical practice in rural New Mexico. In effect, this serves to eliminate what is normally the first phase of professional school education by integrating the knowledge acquisition phase with the knowledge application phase.

Application of Knowledge. This is how Kenneth Bruffee (1978, p. 181) describes the concept of knowledge: "Knowledge turns out not to be some composite, collective memory bank of mankind, but the combination of two mental functions: creative insight and what we traditionally call *judgment.* Creative insight remains enigmatic; it seems inevitably an individual act, and certainly it cannot be taught. Judgment, however, can be taught." He describes judgment (p. 181) as "decision making, discrimination, evaluation, analysis, synthesis, establishing or recognizing conceptual frames of reference, and defining facts within them."

This describes exactly what physicians must do. They must be able to communicate well, listen to patients' complaints, and discriminate between what is and is not important. They must be able to generate a broad set of hypotheses about the possible causes of patients' problems, test the hypotheses, and make decisions about diagnosis and treatment. They must be able to communicate the options to patients and evaluate the results of both the communication and the treatment. In the PCC, students acquire these abilities from the beginning of their professional education in learning group tutorials.

Learning Groups. The typical learning group consists of four or five students and a faculty facilitator. Groups are generally assigned one problem each week and meet for six to eight hours in three tutorial sessions. At the first session, students must acquire sufficient information about the hypothetical patient to identify the problem. Once the problem has been defined, students must formulate hypotheses, which they later use their combined knowledge to test. If their knowledge is inadequate, the task becomes one of obtaining the information needed to solve the problem. As a result, the first session generally concludes with a discussion of the additional information needed, where it can be obtained, and who is responsible for each aspect of the search.

The second meeting typically involves the application of newly acquired information to the problem. Group members discuss how the new information changes the questions that they would have asked of the patient and how it can alter their interpretation of the information. As a result of these discussions, groups often alter their original hypotheses so as to incorporate the new information. This allows new hypotheses and new learning issues to develop as students focus on the cause of the patient's problem and on alternative strategies for managing the patient. As a result, self-directed study between the second and third sessions typically focuses on issues involving pharmacology or other alternative modes of therapy. At the third meeting, the group typically wraps up the issues about the patient. It reviews what has been learned. Sometimes, it even discusses a new problem that provides an opportunity to apply the same concepts. At this session, students also evaluate the problem and their learning process.

Advantages of Problem-Based Learning. Learning the basics by solving patients' problems has many advantages over traditional course work. One is that it profits from the knowledge that students bring to medical school. Another is that it emphasizes the relevance of basic concepts by forcing students to use what they know; that is, by rearranging their knowledge, they learn to apply it to a new situation (Schmidt, 1982). A third advantage of the process is that students must learn to evaluate their own knowledge as well as that of their peers. Finally, it gives them an opportunity to learn the scientific method while solving problems of the type that they will face as professionals.

The Rural Clinical Clerkship. Another way in which the PCC differs dramatically from traditional medical education is that students receive direct exposure to their professional role (see Phase Three in Table 1) much earlier than their counterparts in the conventional track do. In fact, one of the primary reasons for the development of the PCC was that the school was failing in its charge from the state legislature to train doctors to provide medical services in rural communities. As a result, it was decided to expose students to doctors who practiced medicine in a rural setting. This was accomplished by establishing a four-month rural clinical clerkship between the first and second years of the problem-based curriculum. During this clerkship, each student moves to a rural setting and works with a physician who has chosen primary care as his or her life's work. Consequently, students face many sources of anxiety both on and off the job. After only seven months of medical school, students must deal with a wide variety of problems. They work with real patients in their preceptor's practice. Their primary source of feedback is their preceptor, a full-time health care provider, supported by periodic visits from a "circuit-riding" faculty member, and their families must adjust to a new community.

Preparation for Learning Groups in Medicine. Once the choice to use a radical new educational approach had been made, a new set of concerns arose. The new concerns involved two issues: preparation of the learning tasks that students would tackle in learning groups, and education of faculty to teach in this new way. For students to function as a learning group, they must have tasks to accomplish. At McMasters, tasks took the form of problem boxes (Barrows and Mitchell, 1975), card decks that included patient information (Barrows and Tamblyn, 1977), and simulated patients (Barrows, 1971).

At the University of New Mexico, the second and third techniques were used. However, in some cases, the methods became too complex. Students became so involved in interviewing the patient that they were unable to make optimal use of the reasoning process. This problem was recently solved by using a one-line or one-paragraph description of the patient's problem that requires the students' immediate involvement. Students use this description to define the patient's problem and develop a list of hypotheses about cause and mechanism. Items in this list are ranked, tested, and reranked as the solution is sought. As students work through the problem, they explore their knowledge base in depth, and they develop lists of questions that they must research. Learning groups not only help students to develop skills in problem solving but, more importantly, they actually involve students in a problem-based learning process. Elsewhere, Schmidt (1982) develops these concepts in depth.

Preparation of Facilitators. To accomplish the changes in learning modes, the medical educator must assume a significantly different role, becoming a supporter, facilitator, role model, challenger, and motivator of student learning. At McMaster, faculty recognized that their role would change markedly and set about recruiting faculty who supported the concept. The facilitator role, however, still requires preparation and education. This preparation is provided by experiential training involving simulated learning groups. Faculty members are introduced to the concepts of learning groups and student-centered learning through a discussion of group dynamics. Next, they explore ways of getting their own learning group "activated" to accomplish its tasks, and they are presented with a variety of simulated group problems that provide opportunities to practice different interventions. Finally, they take turns acting as facilitator for a group of experienced medical students, and there are critiques both by their peers and by students.

Results. Although the number of participants have been small, experience demonstrates that the PCC can prepare students with adequate content. PCC student scores on National Board Exams, Part I, were the same as those of matched controls in the conventional track in all areas except anatomy, where PCC students scored lower. Possibly more important, however, PCC students maintained a more positive attitude toward the sciences basic to medicine throughout their first two years of medical school, and they were less cynical than their peers in the conventional track (West and others, 1982). Thus, after the first two years of medical school, students on the conventional track had a slightly higher understanding of basic concepts, but the attitudes and the problem-solving and social skills developed by PCC students left them much better prepared for tasks that they would be required to perform both in the later stages of medical school and as practicing physicians.

Learning Groups in Business Education

The ultimate test of the effectiveness of any business school education program is whether its graduates are able to function effectively on the job. As a result, students must not only acquire conceptual skills, such as the ability to understand profit-and-loss statements; they must also be able to use basic information of many kinds to make business decisions. In addition, they must be able to coordinate with and often to supervise the work of others. As a result, besides teaching basic concepts and facts, business educators must provide opportunities that enable students to develop problem-solving and interpersonal skills.

Preinstructional Minitests: Background. During the past few years, an approach developed at the University of Oklahoma has proved to be a practical and effective method of integrating the knowledge acquisition and knowledge application phases of the business curriculum. This approach also helps students to learn to work together as members of a problem-solving group. It is based on the use of individual and group preinstructional minitests that allow application-oriented material to be introduced into courses that normally are devoted almost exclusively to the teaching of basic concepts.

The preinstructional minitest process was developed as part of the team learning instructional format for a course in organizational behavior (Michaelsen, Watson, Cragin, and Fink, 1982). Subsequently, it was modified for courses in accounting, business policy, computers, and statistics. The courses in which the minitest process has been used share certain features: permanent, heterogeneous work groups; reduced reliance on lectures; and grading based on a combination of individual performance, group performance, and peer evaluation. In professional school courses, there is frequent use of application-oriented activities (for example, cases in business policy, problems or projects in accounting and computers).

As part of the introduction to courses in which preinstructional minitests are used, students are assigned to permanent work groups. They are told that homework assignments will be the major vehicle for achieving familiarity with basic concepts; that minitests and subsequent application-oriented assignments will provide them with information on their understanding of concepts and help the instructor to identify topics requiring clarification; and that minitests will be given at the beginning of each major topic area. Most instructors give between six and twelve minitests per term. Often, the first minitest is scheduled for the beginning of the second class meeting.

The Process. The activity sequence followed in the minitest process is depicted in Figure 1: Individual study is followed by individual exam, group discussion and exam (plus scoring of individual and group exams), focused restudy in preparation of "appeals," and pinpointed lectures by the instructor. This activity sequence capitalizes on many of the positive features of personalized systems of instruction (PSIs) while maintaining the cost and motivational advantages of teaching in a classroom setting. For example, the minitest process follows an activity sequence similar to that used in PSIs, but students get

Figure 1. Team Learning Instructional Activity Sequence

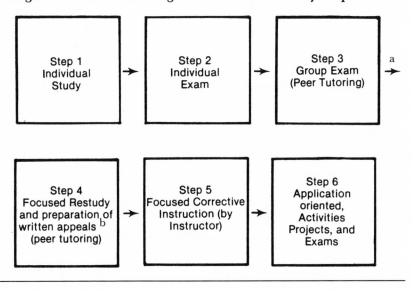

aPreliminary scoring of exams
bWe accept appeals only from groups, but if an appeal is granted, it also counts for the group members' individual exams.

feedback from groups, not a student proctor. Unlike PSIs, however, minitests are given in a classroom setting, and the instructor is personally and actively involved in the examination and feedback process (Michaelsen, Watson, and Fink, 1982).

Results. The minitest process typically has positive effects on both student performance and student attitudes. Scores on individual minitests — generally given before either the instructor's lectures on the in-class group discussions — have averaged between 65 and 70 percent, which is only 10 to 15 percent below student scores on similar questions used in midterm and final exams by the same instructors in previous courses. The minitest process also has positive effects on subsequent application-oriented assignments and projects and on performance on midterm and final exams (Jones, 1982; Michaelsen, Watson, Cragin, and Fink, 1982; Wilson, 1982).

Students are generally positive about the minitest process. In fact, students frequently comment in their evaluations of courses that use minitests that this was the first time they ever enjoyed taking exams. Students have cited six reasons for their positive reactions to the minitest process: It gives them an incentive to keep up with the class. They receive immediate feedback on how well they are doing. They experience a sense of accomplishment from the group exam even if they miss several questions on the individual test. They are rewarded for work done outside class (instead of being bored while the instructor goes over the same material). They learn that group discussions can be a reliable source of information. Finally, they develop friendships with class members (Jones, 1982; Michaelsen, Watson, Cragin, and Fink, 1982).

One reason for the success of the minitest process is that it measurably increases student preparation before class. In part, this occurs because it makes the level of each member's preparation apparent to his or her peers. Student preparation helps to determine the quality of the group's performance. As a result, a student's relationship with other members of the group often becomes more important than grades in determining whether the student completes the homework assignments.

Another reason for the effectiveness of the minitest process is that it provides students with multiple sources of immediate feedback and focused corrective instruction. Much of the feedback and corrective instruction comes from peers and occurs as the groups work on the exams. (Group minitest scores consistently average between 90 to 95 percent in every discipline in which the minitest process has been used.) Additional feedback and corrective instruction is provided by initial scoring of the exam, focused restudy during preparation of appeals, and subsequent comments by the instructor. In addition, more than 90 percent of the group scores are higher than the highest individual score in the group, which shows that even the best students learn from their peers. The overall effect of the increased feedback and focused corrective instruction is to narrow the range and increase the depth of students' understanding to a level that is often above the initial understanding of the best students in the class.

The minitest process also helps instructors to improve their performance. Following the minitests, group discussions, and preparation of appeals, instructors have a great deal of information not only about the concepts that remain unclear but also about the exact nature of students' misunderstandings. By carefully designing questions and by listening to group discussions, instructors can determine what is going on in students' minds. This makes it possible for instructors to focus their lectures precisely in order to meet students' learning needs and to avoid talking over their heads or wasting time on concepts that already have been mastered.

Development of Problem-Solving Skills. Probably the greatest advantage of preinstructional minitests in business courses is that they allow instructors to incorporate applications into courses that normally are devoted to basic concepts. This serves to eliminate one major problem of the knowledge acquisition phase of professional school programs: Students leave such courses not only with a sound understanding of basic conceptual material but also with an appreciation of its usefulness in the larger scheme of things. In addition, since the majority of class time can be devoted to the development of problem-solving skills even in basic courses, students are better prepared to face the challenges of the next two phases of the program.

Learning Groups and the Development of a Professional Role

The final, integrative phase is probably the most challenging aspect of professional school education. During this phase, students participate in situations — integrative courses, simulations, internships — in which they are expected to pull the pieces of their education together in order to fill a professional role. As a result, the tasks that they perform require a great deal of self-confidence (Williamson and Hudspeth, 1982). The tasks also require an ability to interact effectively with consumers, clients, patients, and other professionals. Finally, the learning must occur under circumstances that are likely to create high levels of anxiety in students. Some of the most common sources of anxiety that students confront in this phase are the focus on failures that is inherent in the weeding-out process, the challenge of complex problems, and unfamiliar physical and social settings (Glasser, 1969; Williamson and Hudspeth, 1982). The learning group programs in medicine and business described in this chapter can reduce or eliminate much of this anxiety, which can be a major barrier to learning.

Anxiety About Mistakes. Both problem-based learning and preinstructional minitests tend to build students' confidence while they learn basic concepts. The problem-based learning in the PCC builds student confidence for two reasons: First, it places the focus on discovering the whys of a problem; there is almost no emphasis on right and wrong answers. Second, students acquire the ability to search out answers when they face a problem. As a result, when they face complex problems, they can concentrate on the big picture, because they worry less about solving the individual components of the problem (Williamson and Hudspeth, 1982; Woods and others, 1979). With the prein-structional minitest, the potential negative impact of an occasional low test score is moderated by several factors: Tests are as much diagnostic as they are evaluative. The immediate feedback allows students to understand and learn from their mistakes. Much of the feedback comes from peers, who also make mistakes; thus, mistakes seem less to connote inadequacy than to be a normal part of the learning process. Finally, students gain a feeling of competence from group successes.

Anxiety About Complex Problems. One of the greatest advantages of problem-solving groups and preinstructional minitests is that they both give students repeated opportunities to practice solving problems. This is extremely helpful for students in the integration stage of their professional school programs, because problem-solving skills can be learned and transferred to other situations (Woods and others, 1979). In addition, groups are generally rich in the resources prerequisite to effective problem solving (Woods and others, 1979). Group members' combined knowledge of basic concepts is generally both broad and deep, and their ability to obtain additional information is appreciable. The capacity to brainstorm allows groups to stay motivated in situations where individuals might become frustrated (Woods and others, 1979, p. 282). The combined experience of individuals provides a basis for assessing the reasonableness of assumptions and proposed courses of action, and group members quickly become adept at communicating answers. As a result, far from having to water down problems so that they become less difficult, instructors who use learning groups can use complex problems and let students grow into their professional roles through a series of successes in which they play an increasingly large part.

Anxiety About Unfamiliar Settings. The extensive group work in both the PCC program and the preinstructional minitests helps to reduce much of the anxiety that stems from new settings (Woods and others, 1979). First, working in a group gives students the opportunity to compare their abilities with others'; this helps to alleviate anxiety about being able to meet professional school expectations (Singer and Shockley, 1965). Second, groups provide a readily available source of information that can eliminate potential sources of anxiety outside the course work (for example, coping with the university bureaucracy, parking problems). Third, group membership is by itself anxiety reducing (Shaw, 1981, p. 95).

Probably the greatest contribution of both the PCC and the minitests to the reduction of student anxiety is that they give students a great deal of practice in working intensively with other people in a problem-solving context. As a result, students become better prepared to face the one source of anxiety — working with others — present in every new situation that they enter in the context of a professional role.

Outcomes. Both the primary care curriculum and the preinstructional minitests appear to be highly effective in developing students' ability to perform in a professional role. For example, at the end of a pediatric clerkship, eighteen faculty members at the University of New Mexico evaluated students' performances in basic science knowledge, clinical skills, enthusiasm for learning, ability to work independently, ability to work with others, and maturity. In all areas, PCC students were judged to be significantly better than peers on the conventional track, with the most striking differences in enthusiasm, ability to work independently, and maturity (Duban and others, 1980). Similarly, data from business school courses at the University of Oklahoma in which minitests were used are quite impressive. Even in very large classes of 120 students and more, students' ratings of their progress on developing decision-making and problem-solving skills and on developing skills and viewpoints needed by professionals in the field have consistently been above the ninetieth percentile (Michaelsen, Watson, and Fink, 1982).

Conclusion

The two programs described in this chapter exemplify both the versatility and the effectiveness that learning groups can have in professional school education. The basis for the effectiveness of learning groups is the same, whether they are used to restructure the system completely, as the PCC does, or simply to modify individual courses, as the use of preinstructional minitests does. Learning groups provide a practical and effective means for students to practice skills that they need for professional roles. Through properly designed and supervised group activities, the classroom can become a laboratory in which students can learn both to define and solve problems and develop interpersonal skills. Students become teachers as they grow into professional competence.

54

References

Barrows, H. S. *Simulated Patients.* Springfield, Ill.: Thomas, 1971.

Barrows, H. S., and Mitchell, D. L. M. "An Innovative Course in Undergraduate Neuroscience: Experiment in Problem-Based Learning with 'Problem Boxes.'" *British Journal of Medical Education,* 1975, *9* (4), 223-230.

Barrows, H. S., and Tamblyn, R. M. "The Portable Patient Problem Pack: A Problem-Based Learning Unit." *Journal of Medical Education,* 1977, *52* (12), 1002-1004.

Bruffee, K. A. "The Brooklyn Plan: Attaining Intellectual Growth Through Peer-Group Training." *Liberal Education,* 1978, *64,* 447-468.

Bruffee, K. A. "The Structure of Knowledge and the Future of Liberal Education." *Liberal Education,* 1981, *67,* 177-186.

Duban, S., Galey, W., Waterman, R., and Obenshain, S. "Problem-Based Learning in Medical Education — Does It Make a Difference?" Unpublished manuscript, 1980.

Flexner, A. *Medical Education in the United States and Canada: A Report to the Carnegie Foundation for the Advancement of Teaching.* New York: Carnegie Foundation, 1910.

Glasser, W. *Schools Without Failure.* New York: Harper & Row, 1969.

Hamilton, J. D. "The McMaster Curriculum: A Critique." *British Medical Journal,* 1976, *1* (6019), 1191-1196.

Jones, C. A. "Peer Tutoring in Project Teams." Unpublished doctoral dissertation, University of Oklahoma, 1982.

Kaufman, A., Obenshain, S. S., Voorhees, J. D., Burrola, N. J., Christy, J., Jackson, R., and Mennin, S. "The New Mexico Plan: Primary Case Curriculum." *Public Health Reports,* 1980, *9* (1), 38-40.

Michaelsen, L. K., Cragin, J. P., and Watson, W. E. "Grading and Anxiety: A Strategy for Coping." *Exchange: The Organizational Behavior Teaching Journal,* 1981, *6* (1), 8-14.

Michaelsen, L. K., Watson, W. E., Cragin, J. P., and Fink, L. D. "Team Learning: A Potential Solution to the Problems of Large Classes." *Exchange: The Organizational Behavior Teaching Journal,* 1982, *7* (1), 13-22.

Michaelsen, L. K., Watson, W. E., and Fink, L. D. "Peer Tutoring Through Preinstructional Minitests: A Practical Approach to Mastery Learning." Unpublished manuscript, University of Oklahoma, 1982.

Nadler, G., and Seirig, A. "Professional Engineering Education in the Classroom." *Engineering Education,* 1982, *73* (8), 781-787.

Neufeld, V. R., and Barrows, H. S. "The 'McMaster Philosophy': An Approach to Medical Education." *Journal of Medical Education,* 1974, *49* (11), 1040-1050.

Schmidt, H. G. *Problem-Based Learning: Rationale and Description.* Limberg: Onderzoek van Onderwijs nr 113, Rijksuniversiteit, 1982.

Shaw, M. E. *Group Dynamics: The Psychology of Small-Group Behavior.* New York: McGraw-Hill, 1981.

Singer, J. E., and Schockley, V. L. "Ability and Affiliation." *Journal of Personality and Social Psychology,* 1965, *1,* 95-100.

Spaulding, W. B. "The Undergraduate Medical Curriculum (1969 Model): McMaster University." *Canadian Medical Association Journal,* 1969, *100* (14), 659-664.

West, M., Mennin, S., Kaufman, A., and Galey, W. "Medical Students' Attitudes Toward Basic Sciences: Influence of a Primary Care Curriculum." *Medical Education,* 1982, *16* (4), 188-191.

Williamson, K. J., and Hudspeth, R. T. "Teaching Holistic Thought Through Engineering Design." *Engineering Education,* 1982, *73* (7), 698-703.

Wilson, W. R. "The Use of Permanent Learning Groups in Teaching Introductory Accounting." Unpublished doctoral dissertation, University of Oklahoma, 1982.

Woods, D. R., Crowe, C. M., Hoffman, T. W., and Wright, J. D. "Major Challenges to Teaching Problem-Solving Skills." *Engineering Education,* 1979, *70* (3), 277–284.

Larry K. Michaelsen, associate professor of management at the University of Oklahoma, serves on the editorial board of Exchange: The Organizational Behavior Teaching Journal. *He has worked extensively with teachers on the use of classroom learning groups, and he pioneered the development of team learning, a group-centered format now being used in Australia, China, and the U.S. in a wide variety of physical science, social science, and humanities courses.*

Scott Obenshain is a medical doctor, director of the primary care curriculum, and assistant dean for undergraduate medical education at the University of New Mexico School of Medicine.

Graduate education should prepare students for the scholarly world that depends on exchange, on listening as well as speaking, and on exploration of the connections between one's work and the work of others on the same subject.

Graduate Education and Cooperative Scholarship

Elaine P. Maimon

Graduate education is an isolated and lonely experience today, particularly in the humanities. Conventionally, students confront the challenge of developing professional control over the enormous body of knowledge in a given field. Course work can take them only so far. Much of their time must be spent reading in the library in order to fill gaps in the course coverage of material. When the material includes all English and American literary criticism or all European history, the gaps can seem enormous. Moreover, like the mythic character who only got hungrier the more he ate, graduate students see more clearly the abysses of ignorance in their preparation as their reading increases. Only the strongest dedication keeps a humanities graduate student at work through comprehensive examinations. Then, of course, students confront another kind of loneliness, that of intensely specialized reading and writing for the dissertation. Many graduate students find themselves praying with T. S. Eliot: "Teach us to care and not to care/ Teach us to sit still."

C. Bouton and R. Y. Garth (Eds.). *Learning in Groups*. New Directions for Teaching and Learning, no. 14. San Francisco: Jossey-Bass, June 1983.

Many graduate students in the humanities view their fellow students not as a source of support and encouragement but as competitors for grades, jobs, and favors. These students miss the point that the scholarly community that they are seeking to enter is fundamentally a cooperative place. The scholarly world depends on exchange, on listening as well as on speaking, and on exploration of the connections between one's own work and the work of others on the same subject. The reason that so few graduate students actually become productive scholars may be that they are not socialized to join this larger conversation. Graduate programs have failed in this socialization process because there is an essential disjunction between what educators believe and what they teach through the methodology of graduate classrooms.

Many successful graduate students achieve the delicate balance of Eliot's thought by studying together. Informal study groups are probably as old as education itself. Certainly, in graduate schools, where so little time is spent in the classroom, students have craved opportunities to emerge from their library carrels to converse with other human beings about their work. Studying together provides the opportunity. More than that, studying together makes it possible to contemplate even minimal coverage of vast amounts of material. One student does a thorough job on the criticism of the Pardoner's tale, while another surveys the field on the Wife of Bath, and a third takes responsibility for the Miller. The group gets together and literally exchanges notes. The whole is more than the sum of its parts, because exchange occurs.

Graduate students who form voluntary study groups can, while still apprentices, acquire immunity against one of the most widespread maladies of the humanities professoriat: a condition of increasing isolation as the sides of the library carrel become permanently attached to the human skull, like blinders. Professors in the humanities are too often identified by university colleagues as idiosyncratic and difficult to work with. Scientists do much of their productive work in laboratory groups. In the humanities, scholarship must necessarily involve solitary, uninterrupted hours of thinking, reading, and writing. Yet, professors in the humanities must learn how to work within communities. That learning should begin in the earliest stages of their socialization process into the profession, that is, while they are still in graduate school. This process of socialization into the community of scholars is too important to be left to chance.

Although the conditions of the academic workplace have changed dramatically over the last fifteen years, the structure of graduate education has changed very little. Graduate education in the humanities still confines itself to preparation for a solitary, clerical life that no longer can provide a means of livelihood to many trained practitioners. New Ph.D.'s who expect to spend their professional lives working alone on their own projects will find few havens for sustained solitary scholarship. Even those few who gain employment at large research universities discover that an extended portion of their careers involves teaching undergraduates and taking responsibility for departmental and university activities that require the ability to work in groups. Senior professors in English at the University of Pennsylvania and at Yale University, for instance, are now expected to teach no more than one graduate course per year; the remainder of their teaching responsibilities is fulfilled in undergraduate education.

Two Examples

In some respects, this chapter is as much a plea as it is a report. Let us examine, however, some initial efforts to socialize graduate students to the new conditions of the academic workplace at two large research universities, Pennsylvania and Yale.

One case in point is a remarkable new graduate course developed by Peter Conn, associate professor of English at the University of Pennsylvania. Since 1981, second-year Ph.D. candidates take a course entitled "The Teaching of Literature and Composition" (Conn, 1982). In this graduate course, students study literary works, some of which are used as occasions for composition in the freshman composition sections that they lead. Their professor does not merely supervise their teaching; he, too, teaches a composition section. In the graduate seminar, students also read works on composition theory and pedagogy, including articles by Kenneth Bruffee (1978, 1980) on collaborative learning. Most significant, the students do something almost unheard of in a formal graduate classroom: They work collaboratively on literary bibliography and on reports of composition research. This collaborative experience carries over to the methodology that most use in the freshman sections. Peter Conn (1982) writes of this experience: "As far as I can tell, the graduate students found these repeated acts of cooperation to be unprecedented, time-consuming, exhausting, occasionally maddening...and altogether useful."

Collaborative learning in graduate education at Pennsylvania is not simply the creative whim of a single instructor. All graduate students in English at Penn are now expected to enroll in English 886 before they assume undergraduate teaching duties. Moreover, the course is part of an ambitious writing-across-the-university program that has strong support from the provost and the chairman of the English department.

A program of writing across the university has also been the impetus for cooperative scholarship at Yale. There, under the direction of Joseph Gordon and Linda Peterson, graduate students from a number of different disciplines meet regularly to discuss pedagogical practices appropriate to the teaching of writing in their particular academic areas. One of the primary methodologies involves teaching students to share work in progress. In order to teach others to work collaboratively, graduate students practice the methods themselves in their training sessions. Recently, the University of Pennsylvania launched a similar series of training sessions for graduate students who are teaching assistants in Pennsylvania's writing-across-the-university program.

Crisis and Possibilities

Pennsylvania and Yale are responding to crisis in the academic workplace by remembering that a crisis is a turning point, a time when people see clearly that they must make hard choices. The re-examination of graduate education in the humanities is more than a pragmatic, short-term response to the vagaries of the marketplace. While economic situations may have forced the reassessment, inconsistencies in the intellectual premises for graduate education as currently practiced have long required it.

The preparation of scholars ought to draw apprentices into intellectual conversation at its most sophisticated levels. Contributing to the state of the art in the humanities means nothing less than taking a productive role in that conversation. Stanley Fish writes about membership in interpretive communities, meaning in part in the groups that engage in the conversation that defines a discipline at any given time. Periods of solitary study and thought are necessary in order for individuals to make serious contributions to this conversation. Apprentices must learn, therefore, to sit still for long periods during which they read, think, and compose. But as they formulate their own contributions to the conversation, they must learn to share their work in progress in preparation for going public with their work. Vast numbers of Ph.D. dissertations have remained unfinished because apprentice scholars have never learned to enter the public conversation in easy stages by sharing their work with friends.

If we can persuade graduate students that education is an ongoing conversation, then even the publish-or-perish dichotomy makes ethical and intellectual sense. To publish implies that one strives to hold up one's end of the conversation. If one does not make that effort, one perishes as a member of the academic community. The conversation within a discipline is a continuum that ranges from least sophisticated to most sophisticated. Viewing education as conversation also helps to link scholarship with thinking, since experienced conversants should be glad to take time out from a disciplinary conversation conducted at advanced levels to help newcomers to enter the conversation at levels appropriate to them. But before we can expect students to enter specialized conversation even at the lowest level, we must first help students to enter the general conversation of educated people. Thus, sophisticated scholars have a stake in the teaching of composition, first-year foreign language, Western civilization, and other broad introductory courses to freshmen and sophomores.

Broad introductory courses in these areas should also link study in the humanities to the world of public responsibility. Graduate education has to help apprentices to see these connections and to understand that they are not faddish, not merely reaction to a bad job market. Cicero's ideal orator was a person who balanced solitary contemplation and action in the world. Matthew Arnold was both a poet and an inspector of schools. Graduate training in the humanities must help students to connect activity with contemplation. Apprentice scholars should also learn to converse with colleagues in the elementary and secondary schools. The desperate state of education at those levels has a great deal to do with the isolation of elementary and secondary instructors from the academic community as a whole. Apprentice scholars must also learn to talk to nurses, doctors, lawyers, and businessmen and through that conversation to link the humanities to the professions. Ultimately, apprentice scholars in the humanities must learn to communicate with the public at large—a public that shows its need for such conversations through the banal television programming that it supports, through its political apathy, and through its simplistic views of censorship.

Although we talk of a community of scholars, graduate education in the humanities has failed to build on its own positive intellectual premises. Apprentice scholars emerge from their library carrels to confront a scholarly community and a larger world that they are ill prepared to touch. Thus far, graduate schools in the United States have offered only limited preparation for scholars and teachers in a democracy. Until the 1960s, graduate schools trained only an elite, whose members were invited to select yet another generation of elite. Any sense of cooperation with one another or with the world outside the ivory tower was left to chance and to what one learned from life, not to professional preparation. The case is most extreme in the humanities, since they lack the laboratory experience that provides some opportunity for laboratory teams in the natural sciences and social sciences to learn cooperation.

Graduate education in the humanities must change if we are to preserve the substantive worth of humanistic education. Right now, graduate students are socialized to believe that the ideal scholar is one who works alone. The more patience that one has for solitude, the better a scholar one can expect to be. Time spent on teaching, on program development, on seeking grants (except to pay for more solitary study) is considered evasion. In most instances, communication with a wider community is thought to be pandering.

One way to change the prevalent socialization process is by teaching graduate students to work collectively. Such a change will not be easy, since graduate faculty members are reluctant to change their teaching practices. Yet, a growing number of professors may become aware of the work that shows the efficacy of learning groups. In slowly increasing numbers, senior professors are attending faculty development workshops, especially workshops on writing across the curriculum, in which they are asked to work collaboratively and in which they can discuss the efficacy of collaboration in the classroom.

The efforts at Pennsylvania and at Yale are prototypes of further activity elsewhere. If graduate professors create an environment in which students can work cooperatively in the classroom, students may learn, paradoxically, how to sit still to complete the many solitary acts necessary to scholarship. If students learn to converse with their peers, they can also learn how to engage in active conversation with the larger academic community of scholars. As Robert Frost said, "We work together, whether together or apart."

References

Bruffee, K. A. "The Brooklyn Plan: Attaining Intellectual Growth Through Peer Group Tutoring." *Liberal Education,* 1978, *64,* 447–468.

Bruffee, K. A. "Writing and Reading as Collaborative or Social Acts: The Argument from Kuhn and Vygotsky." Paper presented at the Skidmore Conference on Writing and Thought, 1980.

Conn, P. "Combining Literature and Composition: English 886." *ADE Bulletin,* Summer 1982.

Fish, S. *Is There a Text in this Class?* Cambridge, Mass.: Harvard University Press, 1980.

Elaine P. Maimon directs the writing-across-the-curriculum program she initiated at Beaver College, where she is also associate dean and associate professor of English. During the 1982–83 academic year, she is visiting associate professor of English at the University of Pennsylvania, where she is developing a writing-across-the-university program. With four colleagues, who represent a variety of disciplines, she has written two composition textbooks, Writing in the Arts and Sciences *(Boston: Little, Brown, 1981) and* Readings in the Arts and Sciences *(Little, Brown, 1983). In addition, she has advised many colleges and universities on development of a writing-across-the-curriculum program.*

Study circles differ in almost every way from typical college classes, but they seem to work.

Learning Beyond the Classroom

Karen Quallo Osborne

Learner-initiated and learner-controlled study circles suggest interesting possibilities that colleges and universities can use to promote cooperative learning outside the traditional classroom structure.

In increasing numbers, people are meeting in study circles to learn more about specific topics or to solve particular problems. Senior citizens in New York state are studying opera, literature, the Social Security system, and personal financial management. Workers are exploring better ways to do their jobs, use of microcomputers, preretirement issues, and how to coordinate work and family responsibilities. Communities are trying to solve intercultural, urban gentrification, and national political problems. Adolescents are learning skills for obtaining jobs and for parenting, and they are studying human sexuality and drug abuse. These examples from New York state are paralleled by programs in Canada, Britain, South America, and Australia. In Scandinavia, where study circles originated, one out of every four adults participates in a study circle.

What is a study circle? Why are public and independent colleges and universities using them to enhance learning outside the classroom? Can the study circle experience suggest new possibilities for learning to academic institutions?

C. Bouton and R. Y. Garth (Eds.). *Learning in Groups.* New Directions for
Teaching and Learning, no. 14. San Francisco: Jossey-Bass, June 1983.

Study circles are a democratic form of group learning and problem solving. In a participant-centered process, between five and twenty people come together for a common purpose. Working together, they learn from each other by sharing information and expertise. A peer facilitator trained in group dynamics and the study circle concept helps the group to set and meet goals, encourages everyone in the group to participate, and assists in identifying and securing additional resources. Circles usually meet once a week for an hour or two in places that circle members find convenient and comfortable.

Study circles are effective for all kinds of adult learning. Many study circles use study guides designed specifically for use by study circles. Guides provide a framework for discussion and include some content. There are no externally set learning outcomes to be achieved, however, other than such general goals as acquisition of more knowledge about a particular topic or development of better communication. Similarly, there is no required body of knowledge to cover, and there are no examinations and no grades. Participants identify their own needs, learning objectives, and problem-solving methods. Schedules, meeting places, use of materials, and resources are also determined by the participants.

Benefits to Learning

In a world of constant change, one important benefit of circles is that they can help participants to acquire better ways of coping with change, of gaining new information, and of using that information to create new solutions to individual, community, and societal problems. When yesterday's truths are questioned and yesterday's methods are found to be outmoded, too expensive, or inappropriate, people have trouble adapting. Circles provide a way for people to gain needed skills and to fashion new solutions in an effective and nonthreatening way.

Another welcome benefit, especially during times of economic retrenchment, is the low cost of study circles. Circles draw upon the expertise of an organization's or community's greatest resource, its people. Study circles do not need an instructor, study guides can be used more than once, and meeting places are either free or inexpensive. These same characteristics add to the nonthreatening atmosphere in which study circles operate. A circle helps participants to gain confidence in their own abilities, since there is no authority figure with the one right answer. Circles empower the disenfranchised. Often, they result in positive attitudes about learning and change.

Benefits to Colleges

Both the Scandinavian system and the less-seasoned American experience demonstrate the benefits of circles to learners. Similarly, there are tangible and intangible benefits to colleges and universities that offer circles to their constituents. Reaching out to the untapped pool of learners is part of the mission of institutions of higher education. In today's economy, it is also an essential part of the formula for survival. Circles provide a real community service. They also provide an effective and attractive alternative, particularly for nontraditional learners, to more threatening and less accessible approaches.

Another benefit is the opportunity for faculty to provide assistance. On any given day, a circle can look like a traditional classroom, in which a content expert provides needed information to the group. This traditional teaching, however, comes only when the group requests it, at a time in the course of study when the group feels that it is needed. Teachers also provide content through written and audiovisual materials. Often, study guides are written by faculty and staff. Many circles, therefore, not only empower the learner but free the teacher. Teachers are no longer saddled with the awesome responsibility of having to teach everything that their students are required to know, in a prescribed period of time, regardless of the level of students' motivation, ability, or prior knowledge. In circles, the responsibility belongs to the learners. The teacher is there to provide help if it is needed. Of course, these ideas are not new to education. However, they more often remain theory than become practice.

Where Are Circles Working?

Rockland Community College in Suffern, New York, and the State University of New York at Albany were the first two institutions to join the Office of Adult Learning Services (ALS) of the University of the State of New York in a project to promote the use of circles in America. With a $25,000 grant from the Rockefeller Brothers Fund and a dream to make circles as much a way of life in the United States as they are in Denmark and Sweden, Norman D. Kurland, executive director of ALS, began building a support system for circles. By providing training, learning materials and resources, technical assistance, and evaluation services at the local level, ALS nurtured circle programs to success, and new service providers were sought to act as regional resource centers for circle activities. In response to that search, the University of Rochester, North Country Community College, State University of New York at Buffalo, College of New Rochelle, and Adelphi University joined the State University of New York at Rockland and Albany to form the Study Circle Consortium of New York. The mission of the consortium is the expansion and institutionalization of study circles.

The regional resource center approach has been successful both for clients and for colleges. Although circles are primarily a grass-roots approach to education and problem solving, most circles have been sponsored by organizations for their staff, clientele, or both. Approaching organizations with low-cost programs has uncovered opportunities to provide additional educational and training services both to organizations and to members. In this way, new students are found, new relationships are established in the community, and new clients are developed. This process of outreach into the untapped pool of learners is going on all over New York state, and the number of circles increases each year.

Circles at Work: Some Case Studies

Because circles appeal to a broad spectrum of the public, circle programs are initiated by a wide variety of organizations. Working women, older adults, youth, managers, students, health professionals, and parents all participate in circles. In fact, a two-year assessment of circle programs indicates that there is no typical age or socioeconomic group that participates in study circles. With the exception of gender (more women than men join circles), circles attract members from a broad cross-section of New York state residents. Consequently, sponsorship of study circles is not limited to one kind of organization. Health centers, hospitals, churches, school districts, colleges, manufacturing companies, service organizations, banks, public agencies, and senior citizen centers all use circles to aid the organizations, their clients, or both.

In Rockland County, for example, a group of underemployed women wanted to make a change in their lives. They had heard about circles, but they did not know where to begin, so they approached Rockland Community College for help. As a result, circles were formed to study the topic *women at work.* Using a guide developed by college staff and faculty, study circle members explored the nature and value of work, job stereotypes, the law at work, careers and families, voluntarism, career development in the life cycle, networking, and related topics. The guide provided some content as well as a series of discussion questions. Similarly, a group of women at Buffalo chose circles as a means to gain skills in obtaining jobs. In both cases, the women gained confidence in their own abilities, developed strategies for change, and created a support system that could help to see them through changes.

At about the same time, fifty-two men and women who worked for a large state agency began to meet once a week during their lunch hour. They came together as a result of a noon-hour study circle orientation program that asked employees if they needed help juggling home and work responsibilities. The circles grappled with the complex problems created by demands of work and parenting. Within a year, the number of employees participating in the program doubled. Groups explored child development; effective communcation with children, teachers, administrators, and employers; peer pressure; the world of work; and disciplining children from the office. The State University of New York at Albany provided the facilitator training, outside resources, technical assistance, and evaluation services. Child development specialists, films, books, health professionals, and sociologists were all used by circles at the request of members when they felt that such input was needed. The results have been encouraging. In written and verbal evaluations, parents who participated in the program have indicated greater self-confidence, improved morale at work, and less tension at home.

However, workers are not the only people involved in circles. In New York City, for example, a group of retired men and women who completed a four-year degree at the College of New Rochelle wanted to continue to meet and learn but did not want to pursue the master's degree. They found that circles were the answer. In peer-led circles, retirees studied opera, literature, political science, age and health questions, and societal issues. The college provided the training, space, materials, and technical assistance.

The Other Side of the Coin

Circles, of course, are not for everyone, and they are not problem-free. On the average, the dropout rate from circles is about 15 percent. However, dropouts occur only during the first three meetings. Once the circle has developed some cohesiveness, its members usually stick together; 98 percent of all circles complete the number of meetings that members have agreed on.

Another problem identified by studies both here and in Scandinavia is that circles stray from the ideal. Sometimes they turn into informal classes in which a teacher provides both the direction and the content. Less frequently, they turn into therapy sessions or rap sessions without a learning plan. A ten-year study in Sweden and three years of observation and evaluation in New York state indicate that excellent facilitation is a critical defense against either of these dangers.

Consistently, circles raise two objections from potential users: First, circles are a case of the blind leading the blind. Second, circles take too long to reach consensus and to accomplish their goals. In response, it can be said that, it is true that the blind are leading the blind. The strength and beauty of the study circle process comes from the belief that such an arrangement is both desirable and generally successful. People already know a great deal. They are capable of learning what they do not know from one another and from other sources. When a group realizes that it needs additional information, it seeks that information from teachers, books, experience, tapes, articles, and experiments. Adult learning theory consistently supports the contention that people learn when they are ready. Circles are a practical application of that notion.

The second objection to circles is also true. Circles do take time to accomplish their goals. It takes time to establish trust and security within a group. It takes time to identify needs and develop learning objectives and plans. It takes time to arrive at a consensus. In the aggregate, however, all these tasks are part both of the learning experience and of desired outcomes. Process and content both provide valuable information for learners and tools needed to cope with our changing society.

Conclusion

Like most new ideas, circles are not particularly new. The Chautauqua literary circuit began one hundred years ago. Bible study groups, public affairs discussion groups, and Great Books groups have been functioning in this country for a long time now. What is new is the building of a support system for circles, centered in colleges, that substantially expands study circle opportunities. What also is new is that a consortium of institutions of higher education is working in concert to further the concept of collaborative learning and problem solving.

The study circle experience may well encourage institutions of higher education to reexamine their assumptions about the conditions necessary for effective learning. As learning groups are currently being used in colleges and universities, they either fit into the existing course structure, or they replace it with an alternate formal curriculum of their own. Students' choices and responsibilities are restricted by predetermined goals and procedures, authority, and rewards. The study circle experience invites us to question whether these restrictions are always necessary.

Karen Quallo Osborne is director of corporate programs for Rensselaer Polytechnic Institute. Until fall 1982, she was director of the New York State Study Circle Consortium, which is sponsored by the University of the State of New York. In that capacity, she conducted training sessions for prospective study group facilitators.

*The increasing recognition that all learning is a constructive
process calls into question many traditional teaching practices.
Students need the opportunity to formulate questions and
insights as they occur and to test them in conversation
with others.*

Students in Learning Groups:
Active Learning
Through Conversation

Clark Bouton
Russell Y. Garth

The preceding chapters have described a number of programs that
employ learning groups. These programs differ widely in their goals,
students, disciplines, and teaching techniques. They nevertheless share
some common characteristics that are basic to the use of learning
groups. This chapter and the next set forth the conceptions of learning
and teaching shared by those who use the learning group approach.

Simply stated, effective learning groups seem to have two major
elements: first, an active learning process promoted by student conversation in groups; second, faculty expertise and guidance provided
through structured tasks. That is, it is not sufficient to increase discussion among students, and it is not sufficient to replace listening to lectures with problems for students to work on. Both elements — structured tasks and interaction among peers — seem to be necessary for the
true power of learning groups to be realized. This chapter addresses the
active learning process engendered by work in groups. The next chap-

C. Bouton and R. Y. Garth (Eds.). *Learning in Groups.* New Directions for
Teaching and Learning, no. 14. San Francisco: Jossey-Bass, June 1983.

ter explains ways in which faculty members can encourage and guide learning groups.

Evidence of Learning

Perhaps the first question to ask about any teaching and learning method is whether there is evidence that the intended learning actually occurs (and whether there is evidence that any undesirable, unintended learning occurs). A still small but quite remarkable body of experience and research is gradually making the case that the learning engendered by learning groups is real and important. The programs reported in this book have helped various kinds of learning to take place.

The first issue is subject matter content — specific information and disciplinary concepts. Students in learning groups seem to learn such content at least as well as students in other learning situations; also, they seem to cover as much material as other students do. Larry Michaelsen has comparative data from the University of Oklahoma about test scores of students who take the same class in learning groups and in more traditional ways that bear out both claims. Another kind of learning involves generic cognitive skills, such as problem solving and reasoning. Nearly all the authors of chapters in this book think that learning groups help to enhance these abilities. Still another type of learning involves the various interpersonal skills — leadership, communication, and so forth. Skills in this area are often mentioned in statements of the goals of liberal education, but they are rarely addressed in any direct way in traditional classrooms. Learning groups offer one way for teachers to encourage this learning intentionally. A fourth area of learning that learning groups help to promote is learning about higher education. Several authors mention the role of learning groups in helping students to find friends and to share information about life in college. But Bruffee and Maimon also discuss ways in which learning groups help students to face some of the more fundamental aspects of the higher educational community of inquiring individuals. Finally, because learning groups bring some basic learning processes to the surface, they nurture in students that most elusive of all educational goals — learning how to learn.

The reasons for these learning results become clearer when one understands how learning groups work. Some assumptions about learning common to the use of learning groups differ significantly from the assumptions of traditional teaching methods, such as lectures, discussions, and laboratory sessions. First, it is assumed that knowledge is in some way "constructed" by learners. Thus, the active involvement of students in learning is emphasized. Second, learning is seen to occur in communication with others, not inside the mind of the individual student. Dialogue is essential to learning. Third, the development of skills and abilities is seen as an integral part of the acquisition of knowledge. Indeed, both the acquisition of knowledge and the ability to use it effectively depend on the development of interpersonal skills.

Learning as Construction

Traditional teaching practices seem to be based on an implicit copy theory of learning. Like the old theory of visual perceptions, which assumed that the eye transmitted a copy of the object perceived, traditional teaching assumes that a student leaves the classroom with a copy of the knowledge presented by the teacher. As the copy becomes clearer and more exact, the learning becomes more perfect. Under this assumption, attention is concentrated on the teacher's presentation.

The underlying traditional assumption is that knowledge reaches the mind of the student in essentially the same form as the teacher presents it. Of course, students miss some things and they take away imperfect copies of what was said, but they take away copies, not reconstructions or original creations. If the teacher presents the information in a logical order, nothing in principle prevents the student from assimilating it in the same form.

However inherent these assumptions are to traditional teaching methods, they conflict with an understanding of learning that has been developing over the past half century. In studies of learning, in epistemological writings, in cognitive psychology, and in the studies of college-level teaching effectiveness, there is an increasing perception of learning as a constructive process that conflicts with the traditional notion of teaching as transmission of knowledge to students.

What the student listening to a lecture actually hears is not a copy of what is said; it is a construction. Listening, like all forms of perception, is an effort after meaning. This meaning is achieved by connecting what is encountered in any situation with what the person has brought into the situation. The lecture is neither passively absorbed by students as bits of information in the same serial order in which they are presented nor is it received as an intact structure that has the same logical order. What a listener hears is a reconstruction based on the knowledge, experience, interests, and emotions that the listener brings to the experience. In this process, the original message is altered, the logical connections change, some parts are screened out, other parts are changed beyond recognition, and even additions are made.

Students cannot simply assimilate knowledge as it is presented. To understand what is being said, students must make sense of it or put it all together in a way that is personally meaningful. Teachers implicitly recognize this in their admonitions to students to put something into their own words. Too often, however, this is seen as important only to evaluating whether learning has occurred, not as the core of the learning process. It is as if one were to teach a child to talk by having the child listen in silence to others for the first two or three years of life; only at the end of the period would we allow the child to speak. In reality, the child learns in a continuous process of putting words together and trying them out on others, getting their reactions, and revising speech accordingly. Children do not merely copy others' speech but construct their own unique utterances, which, with practice, become progressively more comprehensible to others. Students also are engaged in the process of putting something together. They know how it corresponds to what has been presented in a textbook or lecture only if they have the opportunity to express it to others, get their responses, revise, and communicate again. Traditional teaching practice virtually ignores this in its preoccupation with the presentation of knowledge — what the teacher is putting out, not what students are taking in.

Since students assimilate all new information and ideas to their existing forms of thought, the teaching process must begin there. Learning is not simply moving from ignorance to knowledge. It is giving up one conception of something for another way of conceiving of it. Unless the teacher takes account of students' perceptions, the new knowledge will be acquired as fragments without real comprehension, or it will be distorted by students' efforts to fit it to their preconceptions. Traditional teaching methods fail to provide essential information. A test of what students know about a topic will not enable a teacher to understand how they think about the subject, nor will class discussions. Given the number of students, the limited time, and the teacher's dominant role, students rarely have an opportunity to develop a line of thought. At best, the teacher gets a hint of how a few students are thinking about the material. Only by observing students as they work on problems can a teacher understand their preconceptions and the way they use new concepts and information.

Learning as Communication

The assumption of the traditional teaching method is that communication functions to transmit knowledge from those who have it to those who do not. Given this assumption, the one-way communication from teacher to student that prevails in traditional classrooms is understandable. The questions and comments of students are important, but they only influence this one-way transmission. Traditional teaching methods also assume that students receive and assimilate knowledge individually, independently of others. So basic is this assumption that the inevitable objection to group learning takes form as the question "How can one teach what one does not know?" This amounts to taking "Of what value is communication to learning unless it is communication by one who knows to one who does not?"

The premise of the learning group approach is indeed that learning involves speaking about what we do not yet know. If learning involves the active construction of knowledge, then that process requires an opportunity to speak and to hear the responses of others. Learners, like the infant who learns to talk, do not simply imitate what they have heard. Learners formulate ideas by putting them in their own words, and they must discover whether they are making sense. An optimum context for learning provides learners with frequent opportunities to create thoughts, to share thoughts with others, and to hear others' reactions. This is not possible in the traditional classroom.

On the most rudimentary levels—specific subject matter content—students in learning groups seem to do at least as well as students in traditional lecture-and-discussion and laboratory formats. This success seems due in part to the increased number of teachers, since group members learn from group conversations. Learning groups are kept small to encourage all members to ask questions and discuss answers. Students in learning groups receive assistance on issues with which they need help and immediate feedback on their learning. This is particularly important in large classes—those with between 100 and 350 students. (See Chapters One and Two in this volume.)

Learning groups also increase students' comprehension of and ability to use underlying concepts. Contrast, for example, conventional classroom discussion with dialogue in a self-led group. The group is small enough that everyone can participate actively. Individuals are sufficiently at ease to become involved spontaneously. The students have a problem to solve. They all work on the same material, and they are approximately equal in ability. There is no expert to be deferred to or to indicate the correct solution. They must depend collectively on their own resources to solve the problem. Students are motivated to contribute what they can to a common goal. They are forced to listen to one another carefully, to discover and correct errors in what others say, to accept criticism, and to provide evidence for their conclusions. In a learning group, it is not enough to know the answer. The group member must be able to convince others. Thus, effective communication is the process through which knowledge is acquired. We only come to know something when we are able to find words that make sense to ourselves and to others. It is in learning group conversations that students first become aware of what they think and what they know.

Finally, communication in learning groups is enhanced because all participants are relatively close to one another in stage of development and level of understanding. By contrast, faculty and students are often at such different levels of understanding that they talk past each other.

Learning As Doing

Common to all the uses of learning groups described in this volume is the premise that students learn course material by doing something with it — discovering, communicating, organizing, interpreting, applying, and so on. This situation differs from that in the traditional classroom, where these activities are performed by the teacher, not by students. The active role of the teacher in the traditional classroom contrasts sharply with the passive role of students. It is not surprising that teaching is the best learning. The teacher's activity makes the traditional method a very effective method of learning — for the teacher.

How are students expected to acquire the abilities that the teacher displays? The assumption seems to be that the teacher "models" the abilities that the students are to acquire and that students will later be able to imitate what they have observed. The teacher constructs an argument, analyzes a piece of literature, exposes a logical fallacy, or computes the solution to a mathematical problem. By repeated observation, the student, it is assumed, internalizes these procedures and acquires these abilities. Rarely are students asked to do these things themselves, and, if they are, it is usually only for the purpose of evaluating whether learning has occurred.

There are two flaws in this concept of modeling. First, there is a narrow interval between what one already knows and what one cannot learn except by approach in successive stages. The teacher's performance lies outside this range. For the student, it seems more a display of brilliance or erudition than a modeling of techniques that the student can be expected to acquire. Modeling can be effective only if the teacher is able to determine students' abilities accurately and if the teacher can confine the modeling to what slightly exceeds students' current abilities. A slightly more advanced student in a learning group is a far more effective model than the teacher can be. In addition, the traditional method provides no way for the teacher to know what students are able to do, since it gives the teacher no opportunity to observe them at work.

The second flaw in the modeling assumption is that it focuses on only part of the process. To be effective, modeling must be followed promptly by opportunities for students to practice the behavior that is modeled, and by feedback on their practice. In the traditional method of teaching, students seldom have an opportunity to practice procedures and abilities displayed by the teacher or to get feedback on their performance. There is only one way to acquire skills and abilities, and that is to practice them.

The skills taught most in traditional college classes are the skills needed to solve well-formed problems. The problem is presented to students in a very specific context and in relation to procedures for solving the problem. The teacher assigns problems that require students to master a specific procedure — for example, multiplication, analysis of character and plot in a novel, application of the marginal utility concept to economic data. Solving such tasks requires students only to recognize the type of problem and the procedures that apply to it.

Problems encountered outside the classroom are rarely so simple, and the skills taught in college courses are of little use in solving them. Such problems are frequently very ill formed. One encounters not a problem but a difficulty, and the hardest part of the task is in recasting the difficulty as the kind of problem that one knows how to solve. We do not encounter problems, but situations in which we need to discover what the problem is. Education should be able to help. But in the traditional college classroom, the teacher's orderly presentation of the material and the restriction of students' purview to one person's way of dealing with the material both ensure that students will rarely encounter a situation in which they can practice the broad problem-solving skills that are essential outside the classroom. In requiring students to respond to the variety of ways in which other group members are thinking about the problem, the learning group method introduces some real-world complexity into the learning situation. Group interaction is a process of questioning, discovery, assertion, and critique. It exercises all the critical faculties and problem-solving skills, and the process produces knowledge that the student is prepared to use.

In addition to affecting cognitive learning, the group experience affects attitudes and behavior. Indeed, many stated goals of higher education are aspects of effective social interaction. Paradoxically, these are to be acquired in the college classroom, which provides one of the most rigid and limited forms of social interaction that we can encounter. The learning group method increases the complexity of interaction among students, and it empowers a greater range of behavior than the traditional classroom does. In addition to purely cognitive activity, a number of other functions—decision making, leadership, mutual assistance—must be performed. There are many ways in which students can contribute to the process. Consequently, students have many opportunities to develop their abilities.

Interpersonal skills cannot be dismissed as something that can be learned adequately outside the classroom. The classroom learning group provides a unique context in which students can develop interpersonal skills. The teacher can act as a neutral observer of group interaction and provide feedback to group members. The learning group provides a situation that is rarely encountered, in which members work on a task and continuously reflect on how they are working together. The situation as a whole provides a context in which individuals can both become aware of their own behavior and feel secure enough to explore and practice new behavior.

Limitations and Difficulties

The conception of student learning inherent in the use of learning groups differs significantly from the premises that underlie traditional teaching. This difference is responsible both for the advantages of learning groups and for the limitations and difficulties posed by their use. Learning groups can enhance student learning, but they do this by changing the role of the student in a radical way. Students seldom experience anything but the traditional method, so they take it for granted that that is the only way to learn. Students "know" what a teacher does, and a teacher who does not lecture or lead the class discussion is somehow not doing the teacher's job. Sometimes the teacher is suspected of withholding knowledge that he or she could simply give to students. Thus, some students feel cheated by the new approach. As one student complained, "Just when I've learned to win at the academic game, you've changed the rules."

The traditional student role can seem very comfortable and secure, while the learning group places new and unfamiliar demands on students. Students are faced with new levels of responsibility for what happens in the classroom; they become responsible for others and dependent on others. They are inexperienced in working with their fellow students, and consequently they are ineffective. They have difficulty giving and receiving criticism, maintaining their own focus on the task, and acknowledging and resolving the inevitable conflicts that arise in cooperative work. At some point in the academic term, many students feel discouraged by the demands that the new method places on them. Some students may acknowledge that they are learning more, but these students say that they still prefer the traditional method, because it is less demanding. Nevertheless, the majority comes to prefer learning groups over the traditional teaching method. However, there is always some anxiety about learning new behaviors, and consequently there is always some resistance to change. Teachers who use learning groups should be aware of this.

Student learning groups are not simply another technique that can easily be incorporated into a predominantly teacher-focused classroom. Used in this way, student groups can be useful, but the effort to incorporate them into the traditional classroom asks students to act in two very different and even conflicting roles, and it does little to change the passive and dependent behavior to which students are habituated. The conceptions on which the learning group approach is based differ from the traditional conceptions and result in very different interactions and outcomes.

For the teacher as well as the students, the learning group approach requires some fundamental changes. For many teachers, it provides an impetus for a general re-examination of their teaching goals and procedures, their identity as teachers, and the skills needed in the role.

The authors of the chapter that follows confront the assumptions and attitudes that underlie our traditional teaching and show that the limitations that they impose can be overcome.

Clark Bouton is a professor of sociology at the University of the District of Columbia. He has written, led workshops, and received grants to study the use of learning groups in college teaching.

Russell Y. Garth, program officer with the U.S. Department of Education's Fund for the Improvement of Postsecondary Education, has worked with several projects that experimented with learning groups. Earlier, he was assistant to the president at the University of Santa Clara and staff member for a higher education committee of the California legislature.

The several functions that comprise teaching can be differentiated and shared in various ways with students to enhance learning.

Teachers and Learning Groups: Dissolution of the Atlas Complex

Donald L. Finkel
G. Stephen Monk

The Atlas Complex

Professor A is just concluding the culminating lecture on one of his favorite topics in his field. In earlier lectures, he painstakingly laid the groundwork, explaining each element and placing each detail of the theory in its proper relationship to the others. Today, he carefully ties the various components together to exhibit one of the most beautiful and powerful theories that he knows of. Each time that he lectures on this theory, he more clearly understands its depth and subtlety, and his lectures improve accordingly. Students find the theory difficult, and so he has learned to inject humor, personal views, and dramatic emphasis to get it across. Today, Professor A's pacing and timing work perfectly. He ends just in time to allow for his usual five minutes of questions. He asks, "Are there any questions?" A few students look up from their

C. Bouton and R. Y. Garth (Eds.). *Learning in Groups.* New Directions for
Teaching and Learning, no. 14. San Francisco: Jossey-Bass, June 1983.

notebooks, but nothing else happens. He fills the silence by raising some questions that naturally arise from the theory. Then, he answers the questions. The students dutifully record the answers. One student asks a polite question about a specific fact in the lecture, and Professor A uses the occasion to expound still more on the theory. Another student asks the inevitable question about how much of the material will be on the exam. When the bell rings, Professor A is stirred by mixed emotions. He is pleased with how well he pulled the lecture together—it is easily the best version that he has given—but he is bothered by how little the students seem to have been moved by it. He has enough experience to know what the absence of real questions means. The students probably admire both his performance and the theory. But they do not feel the power of the theory, and they do not grasp how economically it answers so many deep questions. What must he do to get the excitement of his subject across to students?

Professor B is conducting a seminar in her own field of research. The topic for discussion is one of the seminal works in the field. Some students ask her to clarify certain passages, and she is able to do so clearly and completely. Then she asks a question that she believes to be central to the issues that underlie the work, and one of the brighter students responds in a very thorough and lengthy manner. But, inevitably, the student does not understand the full depth of the issue, and Professor B has a strong impulse to correct and clarify the student's answer. However, as an experienced seminar leader, she stifles this impulse and asks the students if they have any response to the first student's answer. Another student says that he disagrees with the first student and proceeds to give his own long and complete answer. Now, Professor B has two shallow and slightly incorrect answers to clear up. After doing so, she asks another question. She fixes her eye on one of the quieter students, and the student responds very tentatively, so that Professor B must encourage him and help to fill in the details missing from his answer. These separate, truncated dialogues between Professor B and each of her students continue until, out of something approaching desperation, she presses one student on what he means by one of his too neat, almost glib answers. As the student retreats into silence, a feeling of defeat overcomes Professor B. The work that they are discussing always stimulates her thinking with the freshness of its perspectives and insights. At each reading, it raises new questions in her mind. How can it fail to motivate a discussion as involving as those she has with fellow students in graduate school? The cause of the dry, ritualistic seminar before her must be herself, she reasons. She has not asked the right questions.

Both these teachers are the central figures in their classrooms. Like most of their colleagues, they assume full responsibility for all that goes on. They supply motivation, insight, clear explanations, even intellectual curiosity. In exchange, their students supply almost nothing but a faint imitation of the academic performance that they witness. Both teachers so thoroughly dominate the proceedings that they are cut off from what the students know or are confused about. For their part, the students form a group of isolated individuals who have no more in common than their one-to-one relationship with the same individual. While Professors A and B exercise their authority through control of the subject matter and the social encounter in the classroom, they lack the power to make things happen for their students. They are both caught in the middle of their classes by a host of mysterious forces — hidden assumptions, hidden expectations, and the results of their own isolating experience. We call this state the Atlas complex.

In this chapter, we first examine the phenomenon of the Atlas complex. In the next section, we describe a third teacher, Professor C, who is very present in his class but who is not caught in the middle. This example allows us to broaden our perspective on the social organization of the typical college course and on the particular hold that it has on the teacher. Finally, we show the many ways in which this social system can be modified to free teachers from the middle without violating their sense of themselves as teachers. Such modifications should broaden and enrich their view of what they can accomplish as teachers. The result should be a more fulfilling teaching experience and a greater sense of what is possible — in short, a dissolution of the Atlas complex.

The Two-Person Model

Most teachers and students conceive of the heart of education as a two-person relationship. The ideal relationship is that of tutor and tutee alone in a room. Classes are seen only as an economic or pragmatic necessity in which one person — the teacher — either simultaneously engaged in ten or three hundred two-person relationships with separate individuals or addresses a single undifferentiated entity — the audience. Teachers who view their classes as an elaboration of the two-person model are cut off from the potential energy and inspiration that lie in student-to-student interaction or in the mutual support that a group of individuals working toward a common goal can provide. Consequently, it becomes the responsibility of teachers to provide motivation, enlightenment, and a sense of purpose. Like Atlas, such teachers support the entire enterprise.

The sense of fixedness that stems from the two-person model of teaching has both a cognitive and a social component. The cognitive component stems from the teacher's expertise in subject matter, while the social component results from the teacher's occupying the role of group leader in the classroom. Teachers invest a large quantity of their time, energy, and hard work in becoming experts in their disciplines. They have a comprehensive understanding of their subjects and detailed knowledge of their subjects' intricacies and skills. How can they withhold these things? And if students do not get the point the first time, what can teachers do but give again or give more? By the very terms of the encounter, students lack something that the teacher has in abundance; thus, every activity in which the teacher does not give this "something" must play a secondary role. Teachers assume that their principal task is one of improving the ways in which they express their expertise: Clear and precise explanation can always be articulated and sharpened; penetrating questions can always be made more penetrating.

The social component of the sense of fixedness derives from the teacher's role of group leader. The literature on the social psychology of small groups (Slater, 1966) demonstrates that most groups in their early stages can be described precisely by the two-person model; that is, each member acts as if he or she were in an exclusive dyadic relationship with the leader. It is a long and arduous process for group members to break their dependence on the leader and to form mutual bonds with one another. But teachers are more than just leaders. Their expertise in the subject matter exacerbates the problem that all leaders face if they want to distribute responsibility to the individual members of the group. The teacher is the very embodiment of the group's goal — the subject matter. There is no doubt that teachers have all the answers. Why should students look to anyone else?

These forces hold teachers in place with their Atlas-like burden of responsibility. They prevent teachers from sharing some of their responsibilities with the group's members. But some teachers do try to make such a change. They allow individual students to take turns at leading the class, they form study groups of various kinds, they try to restrict their role in discussion to that of facilitator or resource person. And, when they encounter the intensity of the forces, they find themselves pushed back into the center by a cognitive force, by a social force, or by both.

The most striking consequence of allowing students to interact directly and collectively with subject matter without the teacher's mediation is that the teacher comes face to face with students' own partially formed and inadequate conceptions of the subject. As experts with carefully articulated and elaborate views of their subjects, and as representatives of their disciplines, teachers are bound to feel a strong personal discomfort in the presence of the kinds of imprecise, loosely connected, unintegrated comprehension that students have of their subjects. Thus, the very act of opening up and listening to students forces the teacher-expert back into the middle, because imprecise explanations cannot go unrefined, because all the connections have to be made, and because final conclusions have to be drawn. In short, the teacher returns to the center in order to mediate between the students and the material.

For their part, students are likely to resist the teacher's attempt to step out of the middle because they perceive this switch in roles as an attempt to abandon responsible leadership. Students who feel abandoned resent their teacher, and consequently they do not develop the enthusiasm necessary for learning. This in turn leads the teacher who tries to innovate and share responsibility for learning to become cynical about students. The primary reason for this sequence of reactions is that when teachers switch from the role of expert to the role of helper, their expertise gets lost. If students have no way to draw on the teacher's knowledge of the subject, it is natural that they learn less. The attempt to break the two-person model and to cause students to draw on the resources of the group can easily lead to a lowering of the intellectual goals of the class, in the eyes of both teacher and students. And since this is usually judged to be unsatisfactory, the teacher returns to the role of expert, and the students settle back into their seats to take in the teacher's illuminating words.

We have described the way in which the cognitive and social aspects of the two-person model keep teachers in the middle of their classes, carrying all the burden and responsibility of the course on their own shoulders. We have also described how the forces that typically operate on teachers, both from within and without, tend to move them back to the center when they try to leave it. People approach teaching with a set of conventional beliefs about the teacher's role that are strongly reinforced by being in the middle. Years of experience then fuse these beliefs into a whole, so that they cannot be differentiated, questioned, or tested. Instead, they form a complex — a monolithic and undifferentiated state of mind that gives teachers so much responsibility for everything that goes on in the class that they cannot move — a state of mind that we call the Atlas complex.

But a teacher who takes responsibility for all that goes on in the class gives students no room to experiment with ideas, to deepen their understanding of concepts, or to integrate concepts into a coherent system. Most teachers agree that these processes, together with many others, are necessary if students are to understand a subject matter. Any teacher will say that the best way of learning a subject is to teach it — to try to explain it to others. Scientists agree that intellectual exchange, discourse, and debate are important elements in their own professional development. Almost anyone who has learned something well has experienced the particular potency that a collaborative group can have through its ability to promote and make manifest such intellectual processes as assimilating experience or data to conceptual frameworks, wrestling with inadequacies in current conceptions, drawing new distinctions, and integrating separate ideas. The evidence that collective work is a key ingredient to intellectual growth surrounds us. Yet, to judge by the typical college course, most teachers do not believe that it is either appropriate or possible to foster these important processes in the classroom.

Professor C

Before we examine how the Atlas complex can be dissolved, we will describe a class that does not have a teacher in the middle and that still benefits from the teacher's expertise. This should show that change is possible — that the forces holding the teacher in the middle are not irresistible. It should also illustrate the point of view that we wish to advance in the next section.

Professor C walks into his class of forty students and hands out a dittoed "worksheet" to every student. The students continue to chatter as they glance at the worksheet, start to form groups of five (as the worksheet instructs them to do), and seat themselves around the tables in the room. Gradually, the noise level falls as students read through the worksheet. Then, it rises again as they begin to engage in discussion with one another over the questions on the sheet. After a few minutes, Professor C joins one group, where he quietly watches and listens, but does not talk. A few minutes later, he moves to another group. After listening to the discussion there, he suggests to group members that they are not getting anywhere because they misunderstand the example given in the first question. He tells them to draw out in pictures what the example describes, and as they do so, he makes clarifying comments. He listens as discussion resumes, then moves to yet another group. Meanwhile, many students are not only talking but also making notes as they do. Some groups are engaged in heated discussion; others are quieter, as individuals pause to think or to listen to a member who reads a passage aloud from reading that accompanies the worksheet. In one way or another, however, all the groups are working with the sequence of questions and instructions contained in the worksheet.

Professor C may seem to be a teacher with no real function; indeed, he may even seem irresponsible. But keeping a class of forty students actively involved with course material with a minimum of direct support from the teacher requires an artfully written set of instructions and questions. Professor C puts all his expert knowledge, his most provocative questions, and his insights about how students comprehend the material into the worksheets. Breaking his own finished knowledge of his discipline down into its component processes, then provoking students to discover these processes takes at least as much intellectual work as a finely crafted series of lectures would require. But, having done this work and set the students to interacting with one another and with the worksheet, he becomes free to perform a number of helping teaching functions as well as to expound, probe, or press on the basis of his expertise. He can also take time just to listen to students. He is free to choose. (For a more complete description of the worksheet approach and its uses, see Finkel and Monk, 1978, 1979.)

Professor C revises his worksheets after watching his class interact with them (this is where listening becomes important), just as Professor A revises his lectures every time that he gives them. The difference is that Professor C bases his revision on direct observation, while Professor A must rely on his own perception of how he has done, supplemented by a few polite questions and test results. Like Professor B, Professor C always feels that livelier and deeper conversation would result it he only could ask better questions. The difference is that Professor C has had the opportunity to be an outside observer of students' conversation without the concerns of a discussion leader; thus, Professor C can gain a clearer view of what actually happens than even most seminar leaders can.

We offer the example of Professor C not as a model for Professor A, Professor B, or any other teacher to imitate. Answers to teaching problems are never easy. The example of Professor C shows that a teacher can be in his class without being caught in the middle. We will use this example to illustrate a principle that lies behind a variety of possible course restructurings and that helps to relieve the teacher of the Atlas complex.

From Roles to Functions

Professor C serves as an expert in his class primarily through his worksheet. Since students focus on it and not on him, he is free to give clear explanations, to press for clearer answers, and to encourage hesitant students. The power of this approach stems from a fundamental differentiation of the teaching functions that make up the role of teacher. When these functions are differentiated and then distributed throughout a course, many of the constricting features that come from the role of teacher disappear and with them, the peculiar symptoms of the Atlas complex.

Brown (1965, p. 153) observes that "roles are norms that apply to categories of persons." In this case, the category is *teacher*, and anyone who fills that role is expected to follow a certain set of norms in his behavior. Moreover, roles do not exist in isolation; they are defined in interlocking sets, within the context of a given institution. In defining the role of college teacher, we necessarily define norms for college student as well. Social life flows smoothly because of these sets of roles. People enter the social arena knowing in advance what to expect; they have to be confident that the range of unpredictable behavior is strongly limited. Teachers who want to teach in a strikingly different way, for pedagogical reasons, usually find themselves crossing the limits of their role, violating some of the rules that define it. Students will be the first to force them back into doing what teachers are supposed to do; that is, into the conventional role of teacher. Thus, the very predictability that we need from roles can become so rigid by force of habit that the roles of teacher and student become overly restrictive and actually exclude the usual needs of cognitive life in the classroom.

Suppose now that teachers focus not on how they are supposed to behave but on the job that they are supposed to accomplish. Most teachers understand this job to involve such things as getting the students to understand a given theory, having students examine certain phenomena from a new perspective, or teaching students how to perform new skills. Each goal leads to certain mental processes that must be carried out. These processes include organizing and synthesizing a variety of specific facts, ideas, and events into a general scheme; engaging the particulars of a context or experience while maintaining a perspective on its general qualities and compressing and crystallizing connections made within the discipline or between a discipline and the area that it describes. Each process requires a different form of work from students and a different form of assistance from the teacher. A teacher operates in quite different ways depending on whether students are to organize and synthesize, to engage, or to compress and crystallize. Even within each mental process, the teacher has to make choices to act. We call particular ways of operating in a classroom *teaching functions.*

For instance, to get students to organize and synthesize specific facts and events into a general scheme, the teacher can perform such teaching functions as asking students to give their current interpretations of the specific facts and events, laying out projects that allow students to devise their own schemes, responding to students' work, and presenting the teacher's own organizing scheme.

In designing his worksheet, Professor C performed such teaching functions as interpreting student misconceptions, setting goals and tasks, and analyzing his subject matter. In his classroom, Professor C performs such teaching functions as listening to students, redirecting them, clearing up misunderstandings, and supporting students. Notice that analysis of classroom roles ties behavior to persons (teacher, students), while analysis of teaching functions ties behavior to tasks that must be accomplished. Some teaching functions can be performed just as well by students as by the teacher. Other teaching functions can best be performed by groups of students or even by combinations of student groups. As we show in the next section, a conscious decision about which teaching functions are to be performed by whom and where can be made as part of the design of the organization of the course.

The perspective of teaching functions makes the strong negative effects of thinking in terms of teaching roles quite clear. First, any role is inevitably confining. Many teachers acknowledge that a particular teaching function should be performed but that it is not. They say, "Such things are not done" or "Students won't stand for it." This is only a way of saying that their particular role does not permit it. And, because the role does not permit it, most teachers are not inclined consciously to articulate what teaching functions they deem most important for their students' learning.

Second, the language of roles itself creates dilemmas about the ways in which people are to behave. Teachers ask, Is my role of teacher one of expert or helper?, as if they must choose between these two roles.

The conflict disappears if the teacher performs functions that require expertise at one time and place and functions that require helping at others. To say that students must be *independent* (bold, skeptical, imaginative) and *dependent* (relying on the accumulated knowledge of past generations) sounds like a contradiction, because it is couched in the language of roles. The adjectives prescribe contradictory norms for a category of persons. But, if we say instead that some of the activities in which a student must engage require independence and that others require dependence, then the contradiction disappears. There is a time and a place for both independence and dependence when each characterizes a mode of engaging in a specific activity. But, as role descriptors they contradict each other.

Third, roles tend to generate their own work to be done, so that the teacher's activities are determined not by tasks but by roles and expectations. Thus, Professor A becomes a performer caught up in such functions as polishing, timing, and motivating, while Professor B becomes a stage manager of discussions who looks for the perfect sequence of questions so that the actors can play their parts.

Fourth, every role includes several distinct functions. When these functions are performed simply as part of the role, they tend to blur and merge; they are performed simultaneously, but none is performed particularly well. In trying to get feedback after he has spent forty-five minutes driving his points home, Professor A is fooling himself. Likewise, in trying to manage a discussion among students while maintaining high standards of rigor, Professor B performs neither function. A lecturer who gives illuminating examples to stimulate students' thought processes and then immediately gives her own perspective to explain these examples can think of herself as engaging students in a particular context and inviting them to form their own view of it, which she will then enrich. But, for students to perform such an activity in fact requires behavior from the lecturer that the students would tolerate. Thus, Professor B's students do not really go through the process, and she really performs just one function, exposition.

Distributing Teaching Functions in a Course

While most teachers acknowledge that their role is confining and wish to perform a wider array of teaching functions, they find that good intentions, even when backed by strong resolve, do not go far to promote change. To effect genuine change, a teacher must first differentiate teaching functions, then distribute them in the course so that the responsibility for learning is shared with students. Only then can the Atlas complex be dissolved. To do this, the various parts of the course must be clearly distinguished so that the functions appropriate to them can be distributed.

When we think of making structural changes in a formal organization, such as a corporation, the candidates for transformation are immediately apparent. For instance, we can alter channels of communication, or change the authority relations between officers, or merge or divide departments. Like a corporation, a course is a social system. However, when it is viewed simply as a teacher and some students, it seems to lack the structural components that a corporation has, and thus it seems to lack candidates for transformation.

To distribute teaching functions, the teacher needs to distinguish three components in his course: specific activities that serve general teaching functions, people responsible for performing these activities, and the "places" in the course where these activities are performed. For instance, a teacher who wants to perform the teaching function of giving his own perspective on the subject can choose among such activities as these: giving a lecture, having students study a few key examples that exemplify the significance of his own perspective, and asking a highly convergent sequence of questions that point to that perspective. Further, there are many choices as to who performs each particular activity. The typical choice is between the teacher and individual students. However, there are additional candidates for this responsibility: Small groups of students working together can take over some teaching functions. In some instances, the entire classroom group can do so. Finally, there is an enormous array of "places" in any course where various teaching functions can be located. The obvious places include class sessions, tests, homework assignments, office hours, lectures, and quiz sections. These can be refined to include such places as Friday's class, critiqued but ungraded homework, files of past tests, required office conferences, and make-up tests.

Once teachers have differentiated the teaching functions to be performed and consciously distinguished the components of their courses that can be operated on, then they can make local decisions about the specific activities used to realize these functions, about who performs each function, and about where in the course the activity should be carried out. With this strategy for change, teachers can preserve existing activities that already serve important teaching functions and test new activities that may be able to take the place of activities that have not worked out well.

Faced with the complexities of the course as a social system, teachers may well wonder how to get started in such a program for change — particularly since, by our analysis, teachers themselves play such a dominant role in the system. Student learning groups, in which small numbers of students work together in a class without constant assistance from the teacher, can restrict the problem of systematic change to a problem of manageable size. Professor C divided his class into small groups that worked together for two hours, guided by the instructions and questions on the worksheet. Professor C performed many of the expert teaching functions by writing the worksheet, so that he became free in the class to perform many helping functions. Working in groups, the students perform such functions as asking and answering questions, giving support and reinforcement, and providing fresh perspectives on the subject. Each small group of students serves other important functions as well, such as providing carrying energy and bringing out low participators. But, the concept of learning group is extremely elastic. Learning groups can be permanent or temporary. They can work for five minutes, or two hours, or even longer at one time. They can be highly structured by the teacher or not. They can be required to devise group products, which are assigned group grades. Or, they can serve primarily as support groups for individuals.

Teachers who decide to use learning groups as part of a class, no matter on how small a scale, have taken a giant step out of the middle of their class, because in carrying out their decision, they distribute teaching functions, which forces them to deal with all the key issues involved in such a move. What concrete activities will be carried out in the groups? Who will have the responsibility for these activities? At what time and place in the course will learning groups be used?

Teachers who feel that a commitment to learning groups is too radical a step can take smaller steps in the same direction to divest themselves of some of their Atlas-like burden. For instance, Professor A could begin by distributing his beautifully polished lectures in advance and instruct students to read them as preparation for class. This puts him in a position to use the class time as an opportunity to serve a new teaching function. Since he is concerned with eliciting intelligent and informed questions from his students and with having a chance to respond to them, he can use the class period for just this purpose. He can have students bring prepared questions to class, where they can form the basis for a discussion, or he can simply respond to them publicly. He can take yet another step and use small temporary groups of students to drive the intellectual processes necessary for the assimilation and organization of ideas derived from his lecture. To do this, he can distribute a short list of conceptual questions along with his lecture, which each group of students can be responsible for answering. Student work of this nature would enable him to perform yet another teaching function: critiquing without grading the students' response to his lectures. This teaching function would not only be beneficial to the students; it would help Professor A to revise his lectures, because it would give him a sharper view of his students' conception of the subject matter.

In much the same way, Professor B could write her telling and penetrating questions out for students to work on as they do their reading. To reduce her dominant role in the seminar, she can choose a small number of teaching functions to perform during class, to the exclusion of all others. If she still feels that her expertise is not being drawn upon sufficiently she can designate a segment of the seminar (the last fifteen minutes of each class or the last class of each week) in which she answers student questions or comments on student answers. However, she must do this in such a way that students see clearly that the expected behavior for this segment of the seminar is different from the behavior expected in the rest of the seminar.

In the preceding paragraphs, we have made a number of recommendations about how a course can be changed by distribution of teaching functions. However, it is important to remember that, as a social system, a course is not just a variety of distinct structural components; these components are strongly linked. If a change in one part of the system is to have lasting effect, the teacher must consider how this change interacts with other parts of the system. Change that is not integrated into the system will either be isolated and nullified, or it will distort the entire system. For instance, if learning groups are introduced, then their relation to the evaluation structure of the course must be made very clear. Exams signal to students more clearly than anything else what the teacher really cares about, and students direct their behavior accordingly. Thus, if group work is to be taken seriously, the results of group work must be tested by exams. That is, there should be a clear payoff to students for putting their energies into the new activity. Similarly, if the teacher deems collaborative work among students to be important and the teacher works hard to foster it in class, it makes no sense to grade exams on a curve, since students see such grading as a clear message that they are competing with one another.

However far one goes in distributing teaching functions, it is extremely important to set up clear boundaries around the various "places" in the course to which distinct teaching functions have been assigned. Places can be marked off by such means as a designated day of the week or time in the day, a different classroom format, a different medium, a different physical location, or a different mode of evaluation. As long as teachers are absolutely explicit about the nature of the different tasks to be performed in the places marked off by such boundaries, they can ensure the predictability of behavior that people require when they drop stereotypical roles. A lecture carefully organized to give a highly polished overview of the subject indicates one set of behaviors for teacher and students, while a class period in which students work in groups on their first tentative explorations of the subject calls for another. A separate class period in which a panel of students presses the teacher with what they see to be the most important questions on the subject leads to yet another kind of behavior. As long as such class periods are clearly marked off, the diversity of expected behavior can create no confusion. There is a time and a place for students to be receptive and passive, curious and imaginative, challenging and doubting. Similarly, the teacher can assume an authoritative voice for a lecture, become a listener and helper in a worksheet class, and answer questions thoughtfully and carefully before a panel of students. As one boundary after another is crossed in a course, teachers and students can alter their behavior quite radically. All flows smoothly—just as long as the boundaries are absolutely clear.

Dissolution of the Atlas Complex

The perception that each course is in fact a miniature social system is perhaps the key to teachers' dissolution of the Atlas complex. The Atlas complex is a state of mind that keeps teachers fixed in the center of their classroom, supporting the entire burden of responsibility for the course on their own shoulders. This state of mind is hardened by the expectations that surround teachers and by the impact of the experience that results from them. A direct assault on the complex is doomed to fail.

The solution that we propose here is indirect. By focusing teachers' attention on their course as a social system, not on themselves as filling a role, we suggest that teachers can take specific, concrete actions that enable them to share responsibilities in the classroom. To do this, teachers must distinguish the various components of a course—the structural parts that comprise the social system—and distribute teaching functions into them.

There is a continuum along which the teacher can make such changes, ranging from small moves that share responsibility with students as individuals, to use of learning groups, which allows small subgroups of students temporarily to assume a number of different teaching functions, to delegation of major responsibilities to the entire group. We have found that the middle course of action — learning groups — is the most effective way to begin, for it opens up a great number of local possibilities for change while allowing the teacher to keep the fundamental structure of the curriculum and teaching intact.

Most teachers start with a small change, which enables them to experience their teaching in a different way and enriches their view of their course as a social system containing diverse teaching functions. This step leads to alterations in their own and their students' expectations of themselves, which deepen and expand their sense of further possible steps for change in the course. Each further step alters both their experience of teaching and their sense of what is possible. Only in this way is it possible to dissolve the Atlas complex.

References

Brown, R. *Social Psychology*. New York: Free Press, 1965.

Finkel, D. L., and Monk, G. S. *Contexts for Learning: A Teacher's Guide to the Design of Intellectual Experience*. Olympia, Wash.: Evergreen State College, 1978.

Finkel, D. L., and Monk, G. S. "The Design of Intellectual Experience," *Journal of Experiential Education*, 1979, *38*, 31–38.

Slater, P. *Microcosm: Structural, Psychological, and Religious Evolution in Groups*. New York: Wiley, 1966.

Donald L. Finkel is a Member of the Faculty in psychology at The Evergreen State College, Olympia, Washington. He has used learning groups in his own teaching for the past ten years.

G. Stephen Monk is an associate professor of mathematics at the University of Washington in Seattle. Cofounders of the Evergreen Summer Institute for College Teachers, they have worked systematically over the past decade with teachers from diverse disciplines to change their teaching.

Like students in learning groups, teachers can benefit from
communication with and support from colleagues interested
in similar topics. Here are colleagues who are interested
in learning groups.

Conclusion and Resources

Clark Bouton
Russell Y. Garth

The authors of the chapters in this *New Directions for Teaching and Learning*
sourcebook address three types of issues: They look at some persistent
problems in postsecondary education, they report on some ways in
which learning groups have been able to address those problems, and
they indicate some of the learning that has resulted.

A number of basic problems — overcoming passivity in large
classes; teaching basic academic subjects, such as mathematics and
writing; developing competence in academic and other professions —
provide the basic organizing and driving force of this volume. But, as
Chapters Eight and Nine suggest, general perceptions of these problems may be inadequate. Conventional assumptions about learning
and about the art of teaching may be fundamentally flawed. When
learning is seen as an act of construction on the part of the learner and
when teaching is seen not as a prescribed and unvarying role but as a
series of teaching functions or activities whose sequence and emphasis
can be varied, then learning groups seem to be one important way of
encouraging learning.

The idea and practice of learning groups are both fairly inclu-
sive, but learning groups seem to have two major elements: first, an

C. Bouton and R. Y. Garth (Eds.). *Learning in Groups*. New Directions for
Teaching and Learning, no. 14. San Francisco: Jossey-Bass, June 1983.

active learning process promoted by student conversation in groups; second, guidance from teachers through structured tasks. Both elements are essential. Discussion without structured tasks can wander into incoherence or meaninglessness. Nevertheless, while problems and simulations can stimulate students to more active learning, the group context is necessary to increase the opportunity for immediate feedback and to ensure that students work at the appropriate level of development. Learning groups can consist of anywhere between two and seven members. They are a significant part of the learning experience, not simply an adjunct.

The use of learning groups, presumably as of all other educational activities, is justified by its efficacy in improving learning. Although the evidence thus far is sketchy, the range of learning outcomes reported is impressive — particular subject areas, general cognitive skills, interpersonal abilities, knowledge about the higher education community, and understanding of how to learn. In addition, at least in the colleges and universities whose efforts are described in this volume, the benefits for faculty — boosts to morale and renewed attention to teaching functions — have also been significant. Such effects of faculty do, we believe, improve the climate for learning.

Our final words are about some paradoxes presented by actual use of the ideas explored in this book. Both discussion and problem solving enjoy widespread use and respect as educational activities. Yet, it is together that they seem to have the most power to spark learning. However, that combination, which is present in learning groups, still seems fairly rare. On the one hand, learning groups appear to be novel, and they are resisted as a radical experiment proposed at a time when experimentation seems a luxury that we cannot afford. On the other hand, learning groups are also dismissed as something that we all are already doing. The irony, of course, is that because much in the use of learning groups is familiar and tested, learning groups can be used by all kinds of faculty, at all kinds of institutions, in all kinds of disciplines, at all levels of education, without external grants and without major alterations in the structure of colleges and universities. But, our understanding of learning groups is still growing. Although almost all the authors of chapters in this book have conducted workshops to assist other faculty members in trying these approaches, public and accepted wisdom about this activity does not yet exist. This book is an effort by some of those who have been involved with learning groups to consider what they think they are doing and why, in the hope that this can help others both to use learning groups and to understand their place in the educational enterprise.

Resources: People

The authors of the chapters in this book are one obvious and important resource for anyone who wants to understand more about particular uses of learning groups.

Clark Bouton	202-282-2140
Ken Bruffee	212-780-5195
Don Finkel	206-866-6000
Russell Garth	202-245-8091
Elaine Maimon	215-884-3500
Larry Michaelsen	405-325-2651
Steve Monk	206-543-1150
Scott Obenshain	505-277-4823
Karen Osborne	518-270-6051
Beryl Rice	202-282-2123

Resources: Handbooks

Some of the individuals just named can supply handbooks or other materials on request:

"Contexts for Learning: A Teacher's Guide to the Design of Intellectual Experience," by Donald L. Finkel and G. Stephen Monk, 1978.

Particularly helpful in describing the kinds of learning situations that professors can develop for students.

Write to: Donald L. Finkel
The Evergreen State College
Olympia, WA 98505

"Cooperative Learning Project Student Manual," by Clark Bouton and Beryl Rice, 1980.

Outlines ways of introducing students to group process and discusses the respective responsibilities of students and teachers.

Write to: Beryl Rice
University of the District of Columbia
Building 41, Room 5-02-41
4200 Connecticut Avenue, N.W.
Washington, D.C. 20004

Resources: Books and Articles

Abercrombie, M. L. J. *The Anatomy of Judgment.* London: Hutchinson, 1960. Hammondsworth, England: Penguin, 1969.

Abercrombie, M. L. J. *Aims and Techniques of Group Teaching.* Guilford, England: Society for Research into Higher Education, 1970.

Abercrombie, M. L. J., and Terry, P. M. *Talking to Learn: Improving and Learning in Small Groups.* Guilford, England: Society for Reserach into Higher Education, 1978.

Bruffee, K. A. "Collaborative Learning." In *A Short Course in Writing.* (2nd ed.). Cambridge, Mass.: Winthrop, 1980.

Bruffee, K. A. "Liberal Education and the Social Justification of Belief." *Liberal Education,* 1982, *68* (2), 95–114.

Cole, C. C., Jr. *Improving Instruction: Issues and Alternatives for Higher Education.* AAHE-ERIC Higher Education Research Report No. 4. Washington, D.C.: American Association for Higher Education, 1982.

  Covers research on many aspects of teaching; a number of these aspects are relevant to the learning group approach. Includes an extensive bibliography.

Collier, K. G. "Peer-Group Learning in Higher Education: The Development of Higher-Order Skills." *Studies in Higher Education,* 1980, *5* (1), 55–62.

  A review of the literature that shows striking results for student learning groups in developing higher-order cognitive skills. Discusses factors that account for successful and unsuccessful learning groups.

Dewey, J. *Experience and Education.* New York: Collier, 1963. (Originally published in 1938.)

  Dewey has had influence on several generations of teachers and his writings are still a powerful stimulus to reexamine one's assumptions about teaching and learning.

Glassman, E. "The Teacher as Leader." In K. E. Eble (Ed.), *Improving Teaching Styles*. New Directions for Teaching and Learning, no. 1. San Francisco: Jossey-Bass, 1980.

Applies leadership theory to the teaching function, especially to the effective use of cooperative learning groups.

Johnson, D. W., and Johnson, F. P. *Joining Together: Group Theory and Group Skills*. (2nd ed.) Englewood Cliffs, N.J.: Prentice-Hall, 1982.

An introduction to small-group process and to the skills needed to work with groups.

Johnson, D. W., and Johnson, R. T. *Learning Together and Alone*. Englewood Cliffs, N.J.: Prentice-Hall, 1975.

Discusses the use of cooperative, competitive, and individualistic learning situations in elementary and secondary classrooms.

Lewis, H. A. "The Anatomy of Small Groups." *Studies in Higher Education*, 1979, *4* (2), 269–277.

Reviews five books on the use of learning groups in higher education and provides a brief introduction to the extensive use of learning groups in British higher education.

Piaget, J., and Inhelder, B. *The Psychology of the Child*. New York: Basic Books, 1969.

Piaget's studies of cognitive development, which have had a powerful influence on all levels of education, have been a particular stimulus to approaches that emphasize the active, constructive nature of learning.

Sharan, S. "Cooperative Learning in Small Groups: Recent Methods and Effects on Achievement, Attitudes, and Ethnic Relations." *Review of Educational Research*, 1980, *50* (2), 241–271.

Surveys methods for conducting small-group learning in the classroom and the effects on a variety of cognitive and social-affective variables. Studies are of elementary- and secondary-level teaching, but they are also of interest to the college teacher.

Slavin, R. E. "Cooperative Learning." *Review of Educational Research*, 1980, *50* (2), 315–342.

Reviews research on classroom cooperative learning techniques at the elementary and secondary levels. Shows that cooperative learning groups increase student achievement and contribute toward achievement of other goals, and compares the outcomes of various cooperative learning methods.

Watson, E. R. "Small-Group Instruction." In A. B. Knox (Ed.), *Teaching Adults Effectively*. New Directions for Continuing Education, no. 6. San Francisco: Jossey-Bass, 1980.

Discusses implications from research and other sources for use of small-group approaches with adult learners and discusses outcomes that can be achieved through structured learner-centered activities.

Clark Bouton is a professor of sociology at the University of the District of Columbia.

Russell Y. Garth is a program officer with the Fund for the Improvement of Postsecondary Education.

Index

Personalized systems of instruction (PSIs), 48–49

Piaget, J., 103

Professional competence, development of: impact of learning groups on, 51–53; and use of learning groups in business education, 47–51; and use of learning groups in medical education, 42–47. *See also* Learning groups

Q

Quiz sections, as center for student activity and study groups, 11–12

R

Rice, B., 31–40, 101

Rockefeller Brothers Fund, 67

Rockland Community College: role in Office of Adult Learning Services, 67; and study circle program, 68–69

S

Schmidt, H. G., 45, 46, 54

Seireg, A., 41, 54

Shaghnessy, M. P., 24, 25, 29

Sharan, S., 103

Shaw, M. E., 52, 54

Skills courses, 31–32. *See also* Students

Slater, P., 86, 97

Slavin, R. E., 104

Spaulding, W. B., 44, 54

State University of New York at Albany, role in Office of Adult Learning Services, 67; study circle program at, 69

State University of New York at Buffalo, 68

State University of New York at Rockland, 68

Students: developing skills and abilities of, 31–39; graduate, problems of, 57–62; passivity of, 20–22; role of, in learning, 80–81

Study Circle Consortium of New York, 68

Study circles: benefits to colleges of, 67; benefits to learning of, 66; case studies of, 68–69; and the community, 68–69; definition of, 65–66; learner-controlled, 65; learner-initiated, 65; problems of, 69–70; where employed, 67–68

T

Tamblyn, R. M., 46, 54

Teaching: functions, 91–92; increasing effectiveness of, 37–38; and learning groups, 94–95; roles in, 87, 90–91; as social system, 94, 96, 99; two-person model of, 85–88; of writing, 25–28

Teaching assistants (TAs), in mathematics courses, 7–12

Team learning: advantages of, 13–14; definition of, 13; and developing and managing group-oriented activities, 16–18; and enhancement of learning, 15; and grading system, 18; and handling disagreements, 19; and instructor enrichment, 21; and older, returning students, 20; and organization of material, 15–16; pacing methods and, 17; primary instructional activity of, 15; and providing feedback, 18–9; and results of use with large classes, 19–20; and student attitudes toward, 20; and use of mini-tests, 16

Terry, P. M., 102

Testing: and team learning, 16; and use of mini-tests, 16–19, 48–50. *See also* Team learning; Business education

U

University of Rochester, 68

University of the State of New York, Office of Adult Learning Services (ALS) at, 67

V

Voorhees, S. S., 54

W

Waterman, R., 54

Watson, E. R., 104

Watson, W. E., 15, 16, 17, 19, 21, 22, 48, 49, 50, 53, 54

West, M., 47, 54

Williamson, K. J., 41, 42, 51, 52, 54

Wilson, W. R., 49, 54

Women's support groups, 3

Woods, D. R., 41, 52, 54

Wright, J. D., 54

Writing-across-the-curriculum program at the University of Pennsylvania, 60